# Rhododendrons and Azaleas

BY THE SUNSET EDITORIAL STAFF

Editor for this book: Philip Edinger

Lane Books · Menlo Park, California

# Acknowledgments

Books dealing with subjects such as rhododendrons and azaleas of necessity contain much information which is best supplied by specialists. It is then the editor's responsibility to organize this information, evaluate it, and finally put it into a form which will be easily grasped by the layman. Special credit, therefore, is well-deserved by a number of experts who selflessly gave of their knowledge and years of experience by checking manuscript and consulting with the editors of *Sunset* so that their special interest might be enjoyed—even avidly cultivated—by numberless gardeners in the temperate zones.

We wish to acknowledge the invaluable aid of Warren Baldsiefen, Nurseryman, Bellevale, New York; Dr. Paul J. Bowman, Fort Bragg, California; Robert M. Bovee, Nurseryman, Portland, Oregon; P. H. Brydon, Salem, Oregon; Dr. J. Harold Clarke, Author and Nurseryman, Long Beach, Washington; Robert Comerford, Nurseryman, Marion, Oregon; Cottage Gardens Nursery, Eureka, California; the Crowells, Nurserymen, Albion, California; Mrs. Donald C. Davis, Bellevue, Washington; Toichi Domoto, Nurseryman, Hayward, California; Walter Doty, Los Altos, California; Everett E. Farwell, Nurseryman, Woodside, California; Fred C. Galle, Director of Horticulture, Callaway Gardens, Pine Mountain, Georgia; James Gossler, Nurseryman, Springfield, Oregon; Roy Hudson, Director of Strybing Arboretum, San Francisco, California; Mrs. W. A. Kelius, Levittown, Pennsylvania; Kramer Brothers Nurseries, Upland, California; Dr. David G. Leach, Author and Lecturer, Brookville, Pennsylvania; Walter Lee, Nurseryman, Monrovia, California; Julius Nuccio, Nurseryman, Altadena, California; Dr. Carl H. Phetteplace, Eugene, Oregon; Ernest Schoefer, Mendocino Coast Botanical Gardens, Fort Bragg, California; A. M. Shammarello, Nurseryman, Euclid, Ohio; Ted Van Veen, Nurseryman, Portland, Oregon; Mrs. G. P. Whiteley, Seattle, Washington. Detailed descriptions of hybrids and species were facilitated by two publications of the American Rhododendron Society: *Rhododendron Information,* and *Rhododendrons for Your Garden.*

FRONT COVER: Luminous beauty of the English hybrid rhododendron 'Pink Pearl' has delighted several generations of gardeners. Adaptability and reliability are two of its outstanding qualities. Flowers shown are about full size. Photo by Glenn Christiansen.

BACK COVER; INSIDE FRONT AND BACK COVERS: Photographs courtesy of Sweeney, Krist, & Dimm, Horticultural Lithographers, Portland, Oregon.

ILLUSTRATIONS by Dinah James

# Contents

# Meet the Rhododendron Clan

## Colorful, distinguished plants from around the world

To meet most of the rhododendrons and azaleas you would have to undertake an around-the-world journey, starting, perhaps, in Washington, Oregon, or California, browse through Appalachia, and then touch down in such romantic spots as Turkey and Armenia, Nepal, Sikkim, Tibet, even Afghanistan, and all of Eastern Asia—from Siberia to New Guinea. Indeed, South-East Asia along the Himalayan frontier of China and her southern neighbors is considered to be the homeland of the genus. Certainly it contains the largest number of species and natural hybrids per square mile of any area that provides a natural home for these plants. Within this territory are intermountain valleys which may contain as many as 200 species, all visible (although not all distinguishable) from a single vantage point!

Yet, with all these native floral treasures, Eastern Asia was the last area to reveal her rhododendrons and azaleas to Western plant explorers.

### Rhododendrons in the Wild

A trip to northern India and into the Himalaya mountains will give you a comprehensive, condensed view of the rhododendron clan, for as you climb higher and higher through several forest types and up beyond the timberline you will encounter most of the variations in growth and flower styles that the genus has to offer. Climatic conditions—amount of rain and snow, the seasons when they can be expected—vary enough throughout the Himalayas and the foothills on either side of the range that no one area can be selected and described as "typical." However, a look at any location there will give you an idea of the incredible diversity of rhododendron flower and plant types and the manners in which they grow.

In the lower elevations (this, depending on the region, may be as much as 8,000 feet) rhododendrons are scattered among other plant types, quite inconspicuous when out of bloom. In our "type" location on the northeast Burmese frontier, the first species you encounter may be growing along —or even in—rocky stream beds. Climbing another one or two thousand feet, you're likely to smell the rhododendrons almost before you see them: whitish flowers that look more like Easter Lilies but which are clambering through tree and shrub branches instead. These are the tender, often epiphytic species which are greenhouse subjects except in the mildest climates. If you look up you may discover to your surprise that you're walking *under* a rhododendron; the first tree types appear in this constantly-moist rain forest.

Another thousand feet or so brings you into the heart of a temperate rain forest with a number of familiar trees: oaks, magnolias, and other broad-leafed types. The tree rhododendrons are still scattered through these, but numerous colorful flowering shrubs in the forest and on cliffsides catch your eye—more rhododendrons. At the upper limit of this forest, more species are found in colonies on rocky ridges, and scrub-forming sorts begin to appear in dense tangles by themselves or interlaced with dwarf bamboo.

Eventually—between 9,000 and 10,000 feet—most broad-leafed trees give way to conifers, predominantly fir. Here you will have to cut your way through thickets and forests of rhododendrons: gnarled trees, scrub and bamboo associations, picturesque plants literally hanging from cliffs and cascading over rocks. If you arrive there in early spring you'll see a breathtaking spectacle of light green and bronzy new foliage, dark bluish-green fir trees, and frothy billows everywhere of

*RHODODENDRONS AND AZALEAS THRIVE in the protection of old Mount Atlas Cedars. In this Northwest garden they get ideal combination of sun and shelter.*

thousands of rhododendron flowers in scarlet, white, purple, pink, lemon—with flawless blue sky overhead.

Even above the timberline, rhododendron thickets 2-3 feet high persist, making travel difficult. Finally you reach high-altitude moorlands where summers may be dry and snow covers the ground for six months of the year. Here are hundreds of square miles of alpine rhododendrons no more than calf-deep, clothing the rocks and meadows in all gradations of pink through purple, with amber and gold for contrast.

Based upon observations made during his several exciting expeditions to the Himalayan region, Captain F. Kingdon Ward determined that the more congenial a climate is for rhododendrons and azaleas, the greater will be the number of species growing there—each one usually inhabiting a small territory. Conversely, where conditions approach borderline, very few species are to be found but they frequently extend over vast areas. Below the timberline in the Himalayas, adjacent

*DELICATE PATTERN of pale green leaves and soft pink blossoms is typical of* R. schlippenbachii.

hills or valleys may contain different species found only in those locations, growing among a number of other locally-distributed types. This is both exciting to the plant collector who can expect rich rewards in terms of new forms or species, yet frustrating to think he may be missing still more spectacular floral treasures which await him on that hill he neglected to explore!

## TWENTY-THREE CENTURIES OF RHODODENDRONS

The chronology of recorded rhododendron history begins around 400 B.C. with an account of Greek soldiers, retreating from a Persian defeat, who became dangerously ill after eating honey made from nectar of the Pontic Azalea (*Rhododendron luteum*) which grew where they had camped along the Black Sea. Three hundred years later a Roman army was badly massacred at almost the same location while the troops were stupefied after having eaten honey from the same source.

Herbalists and pharmacologists in the middle ages knew of the effects caused by eating the honey, also of the toxic properties of some rhododendron leaves which, if taken in carefully-prepared brews, could have some medicinal value in cases of rheumatism or arthritis. The practice of medicine being in the formative stages then, not all prescriptions were unqualified successes. A series of diabolical experiments in Europe with tea made from leaves of the Siberian Snow Rose (*Rhododendron chrysanthum*) closely coincided with the first attempts to bring rhododendron species into the garden for ornamental purposes.

### The Dawn of Discovery

The English, during their days of empire building in the 18th and 19th centuries, were the earliest to collect wild rhododendrons and azaleas and domesticate them. The first exotic rhododendron to reach Britain was from the Alps in 1656; then, 80 years went by before four new species crossed the ocean—this time from the American Colonies. During the remainder of the 1700's an additional seven species were introduced to cultivation, including several northern Asian kinds raised from seed sent by the eminent German naturalist Pallas. The early years of the 19th century found another handful of new species in English gardens; contained in this last group was the genesis for the rhododendron explosion which was to occur around 1830.

WIDE VARIETY of shapes and sizes are available for today's rhododendron enthusiast. This Tibetan dwarf, R. pemakoense, grows less than a foot high, produces lavender-pink blooms in April.

The American *Rhododendron catawbiense*, which annually decorates the Appalachian mountains in clouds of pink, mauve, and lavender, arrived in England from North Carolina in 1809. Although color purists criticize the amount of blue in its pink flowers, the Catawba Rhododendron produces these blooms in large rather compact trusses and—most importantly—on a very hardy, adaptable, attractive shrub. The pioneer British hybridizer Michael Waterer anticipated its value the year after its introduction and crossed it with the other large Eastern-United States native —*Rhododendron maximum*. Here was the first careful attempt to guide rhododendron evolution.

The other species which was to fire the imagination of rhododendron enthusiasts was sent to England in 1811: This was *Rhododendron arboreum*. A tree in its native India, it was also the first of the South-East Asian species that English gardeners were given a chance to grow. Fourteen years after its introduction to cultivation the first plants flowered—in dazzling scarlet.

**East Meets West in Early Hybrids**

Because *Rhododendron arboreum* was too tender for all but the warmest coastal gardens in the British Isles, several hybridizers attempted to combine the spectacular red color with a hardier plant; the first crosses were made with the Catawba Rhododendron and several of its earlier hybrids. That the efforts were in a measure successful is proved by the deep pink and red hybrid seedlings which first flowered several years later, yet are still to be found in some gardens today.

The real importance of these first hybrids, however, was that they demonstrated what possibilities lay ahead. Even in first generation seedlings from a tender sub-tropical species, hybridizers were able to capture much of the color they sought while making these colors available to gardeners on plants which could endure some winter cold.

The possibilities for development were exciting, and this excitement proved to be an impetus to explore British India for more exotics to enrich the hybridizers' reservoir of materials. Rising to the occasion, Sir Joseph Hooker scouted the area of Sikkim and in 1850 sent back 45 newly-discovered species which he also presented in a meticulously beautiful publication, *Rhododendrons of the Sikkim Himalaya*.

New species continued to be discovered (mostly in Asia) and introduced throughout the rest of

CLEAR PURPLE FLOWERS cluster above metallic, bronze-green leaves of the dwarf R. russatum.

the century until by 1900 some 300 were in cultivation. It was also during the last half of the nineteenth century that many hybrids originated which even today constitute the mainstay of standard, satisfactory garden rhododendrons—'Cynthia,' 'Pink Pearl,' and 'Sappho,' to name only a few.

## Developments with Azaleas

Numerous American native azaleas (all deciduous) had reached England by 1800—enthusiastically sent there by collectors who ranged from the New England seaboard to the southern Gulf Coast and throughout the Appalachian Mountains. By this time, too, the notorious Pontic Azalea (Rhododendron luteum) was in cultivation there. The East India companies of Great Britain and Holland brought a number of Asian azaleas (both deciduous and evergreen) to Europe during the 18th and 19th centuries, including some Japanese species

(via China or Indonesia) even though Japan itself was closed to trade with the western world.

By the 1820's azalea hybridizers had many more species with which to experiment than did the rhododendron enthusiasts, and so hybrid seedlings began appearing with increasingly complex parentages. At first, Belgium led the other countries in production of new varieties—remembered today by the evergreen Belgian Indica hybrids and the deciduous Ghent hybrids. Throughout the century new species were brought to Britain, Belgium, and Holland from the Orient and were generally incorporated into hybridizing programs. As more and more collections were made, it was discovered that a number of Oriental "species" were actually natural hybrids, variants of several widespread species, or Old Japanese garden hybrids developed there during Japan's centuries of isolation. Conversely, American species sent to Europe in several cases turned out to include more than one species under a single name. While ancestries of evergreen and deciduous azaleas are complex, the confusion of parent stock makes it difficult to sort out exact hybrid backgrounds.

The introduction to England of America's Western Azalea (Rhododendron occidentale) in the mid-1800's added a new dimension to deciduous azalea breeding which is noticeable to this day. Combined with hybrids of the Chinese and Japanese deciduous azaleas (with, sometimes, the inclusion of Appalachia's Flame Azalea), the yellow, orange, and red hybrids branched out to include softer pinks, salmon, cream, and white and many began to assume a "square" appearance to the flower. Today's Knap Hill, Exbury and similar strains reveal the influence of Rhododendron occidentale flower form in all colors from white through red. By 1900 the basic parent stock of present deciduous hybrids had been assembled and combined.

## Twentieth-Century Population Explosion

With some 300 rhododendron species and numerous hybrid varieties available at the turn of the century, it appeared that gardeners and hybridizers alike had at their disposal almost more than enough material to satisfy their horticultural and experimental desires. Few would have imagined that plant-hunting expeditions during the first two decades of the 1900's would reveal that only about one-third of the world's rhododendrons had been described and introduced to cultivation.

The first of these explorers to realize the extent of what awaited discovery was Ernest H. Wilson. Hired by an English nursery to search for the fabled Dove Tree in China, he ran into incredibly varied rhododendrons in the western Chinese provinces—sending back from his first expedition nearly as many new species as Hooker had 50 years earlier. Wilson made three subsequent expeditions, each as successful as the first.

Other courageous, dedicated, determined men in the employ of various nurseries, arboretums, or foundations similarly immortalized themselves through the quantity and quality of their discoveries in China, Burma, Tibet, and Bhutan. It is still exciting to imagine the thrill of being the first Westerner—knowing what value these new plants could have to horticulture—to glimpse as did F. Kingdon Ward a miles-high moorland in Western China covered with alpine rhododendrons in "a chromatic storm-tossed surf—rose, pink, purple, lavender, and amber, through which one may wade ankle deep for days on end."

## Order Amid Chaos: The Series Concept

Eventually confronted by somewhere between 700 and 900 species which ranged from heath-like ground covers to tropical-looking trees—very different from one another in appearance but distressingly similar botanically—amateurs, specialists, and botanists alike recognized the need for arranging these species in a system which would acknowledge their similarities but categorize the differences. Azaleas had always presented a classification problem, from the time of Linnaeus who, in 1753, attempted to classify all known plants. With so few rhododendron and azalea species available for his observation, his solution was to put azaleas in a separate genus. As a group, azaleas do have some characteristics not shared with other rhododendrons, but there are still enough similarities that the two will hybridize—although the resulting "azaleodendrons" are sterile. And then there are some rhododendrons which, at first glance, *look* like azaleas. Compounding the overall problem was the ease with which adjoining species hybridized in the wild; the taxonomists (those botanists responsible for plant classification) first had to determine that what they were trying to describe and classify were species rather than natural hybrids.

Out of this confusion came an ingenious solution devised by Sir Isaac Bayley Balfour, who also

*BRILLIANT FALL FOLIAGE of* R. mucronulatum *is followed in earliest spring by rose-purple blossoms.*

*DRAMATIC FOOT-LONG LEAVES of the Nepalese R. falconeri are foil for purple-spotted creamy flowers.*

*BILLOWS OF LAVENDER-BLUE BLOSSOMS, from light to deep violet, characterize the Chinese R. augustinii.*

classified those alpine rhododendrons from Kingdon Ward's storm-tossed chromatic surf. What he did was divide the genus *Rhododendron* into a number of *series*, each of which contained from one to many species which appeared to be closely related. Each series was given the name of a prominent species contained therein. Often, where many species were grouped in one series, they were further differentiated into smaller, more closely-knit *sub-series* within the series. This system finally accommodated the azaleas comfortably: in their own series. You could then mention with assurance *Rhododendron indicum* 'Duc de Rohan', yet with equal correctness call it an azalea in reference to the series Azalea.

Today there are 43 series. Although classification of species may change and specific status may be granted or withdrawn as rhododendron research continues, the overall organization created by Balfour can accommodate such change.

### The Men Behind the Hybrids

The reputation of rhododendrons as a rich man's flower is not entirely unfounded, but not because they are so difficult to grow or so initially expensive that it requires money to have them. Rather, it was the wealthy and titled persons of the nineteenth and early twentieth centuries who had the time to grow and develop these plants, the land on which to do it (most of the earlier rhododendron hybrids and their parent species were *large* shrubs), and the money to hire gardeners to attend large collections of plants. Perhaps the most outstanding person in this category was the late Lionel de Rothschild who assembled the world's largest (and possibly finest) rhododendron collection at his Exbury estate in England. With the best materials at his disposal and guided by impeccable taste, he produced numerous hybrids outstanding for their refinement and quality.

The professional nurserymen, however, were for nearly a century responsible for the bulk of the hybrid output. A glance at listings of standard hybrids will repeatedly disclose the names of Waterer and Slocock in England, Koster and Van Nes in Holland. Since the concern of these nurserymen was necessarily commercial as well as artistic, their hybrids tended to stress certain commercial advantages: easy to propagate; tough, adaptable, well-foliaged plants; vigorous, trouble-free growth, with large flowers clustered in showy compact trusses.

Although azaleas were plantation favorites in the Southern United States, it was rare indeed (until recently) for rhododendrons or azaleas to be enjoyed in this country on the scale that they were in Europe—especially in Great Britain, where winters are generally mild enough to allow gardeners a large selection of hybrids. To the Waterer family in particular must go the credit for developing showy rhododendron hybrids which could endure winters cold enough to provide spring color in inland locations north of New York City and in other eastern areas devoid of moderating coastal influences.

## IN THE FUTURE

Rhododendrons and azaleas can only gain in popularity as gardeners discover the variety of colors and forms available to them and become familiar with basic cultural guidelines. Here are three trends which are significantly contributing to the popularity of these plants.

**Emphasis on smaller plants.** During the first two decades of this century the Asian rhododendron discoveries vastly expanded concepts of possibilities for different colors, plant forms, and flower carriage as compared to traditional values represented by English and Dutch nursery hybrids. Contained in the flood of new species were not only alpines and forest giants, but numerous species of small to intermediate size—smaller-leafed than the nursery hybrids and with flowers carried in informal clusters. These have been taken in hand by a number of contemporary hybridizers who are concerned with developing smaller plants which will fit more comfortably into the ever-shrinking suburban garden. Fine as are many of the time-tested hybrids, they lose some appeal where they are obviously out of scale in a garden.

**Select parent material.** Continued explorations coupled with extensive culture of species from seed have demonstrated the variability inherent in most species and the importance of using fine selected forms in hybridizing programs. Selections of numerous species are offered in the nursery trade; these may be superior color variants, clones which flower more freely than the usual, or plants with better growth habits. A classic example of the value in choosing superior forms for parent material is the superb assemblage of varieties in the 'Loderi' group: Their originator, Sir Edmund Loder, carefully selected the finest obtainable

forms of *Rhododendrons griffithianum* and *fortunei* and produced from them, around 1901, a number of still-unsurpassed hybrids.

**Increased cultural knowledge.** The research and advancement in rhododendron and azalea knowledge is continually pushing cultural frontiers into areas once thought inhospitable to these plants. As adventuresome gardeners continue to experiment in these areas, varieties will be discovered which will adapt themselves admirably to less-friendly conditions. The increase in popularity of rhododendrons in the southern states—where soil fungi were presumed to be a limiting factor—is proof that cultural obstacles can be overcome. Similarly, the problems of central Californian heat and southern Californian alkaline water can now be handled in ways which allow gardeners in those areas to enjoy rhododendrons and azaleas as permanent landscape features.

Adding to the weight of the previous three points is the increasing number of people who are becoming actively involved with rhododendrons and azaleas. Today, the development of these plants is in the hands of many dedicated amateurs as well as professional growers and in nearly all areas of the world where they will grow.

*PACIFIC COAST NATIVE,* R. macrophyllum *grows with its foliage in sunlight but its roots in shade.*

*NATIVE TO CHINA is* R. racemosum; *it displays 1-inch pink flowers on dwarf to very tall plants.*

*FROM THE HIMALAYA MOUNTAINS comes* R. ciliatum *with its 2-inch white blossoms and dark, hairy leaves.*

*HYBRID of the two Asian species is 'Racil,' having the characteristics of both parents.*

## A RHODODENDRON GLOSSARY

The botanical world has its own unique dictionary of descriptive terms—words which take on special meaning when used in connection with plants, or words especially coined for them. Here are a number of terms which you will encounter in rhododendron literature.

**Clone:** a plant which has been propagated by cuttings, layers, or grafts from a single original plant, and is therefore invariable. This may refer to a species or a hybrid.

**Cultivar:** literally, "cultivated variety"; a single *hybrid* clone propagated from cuttings, layers or grafts—and therefore invariable.

**Genus:** a group of closely related species, clearly different from other such groups.

**Group (grex):** a name assigned to a *cross* rather than to individual superior hybrids from the cross. All seedlings of that cross produced by anyone, anywhere, are entitled to the group name (e.g. the 'Loderi' group of hybrids), regardless of their quality. To distinguish one superior seedling in a group from another, individual names may be assigned (e.g. Loderi 'King George,' Loderi 'Venus'). This system was practiced chiefly in Great Britain and is now discouraged.

**Hybrid:** any rhododendron or azalea which resulted from cross-fertilization of two other individuals. Hybrids may have been planned and produced by a hybridizer or may have occurred in the wild (known, then, as a "natural hybrid").

**Indumentum:** the hairy coating often found on the underside of rhododendron leaves.

**Seedling:** a plant raised from seed but which does not have a clonal or hybrid name. This may apply to species and hybrids alike.

**Series:** artificial divisions of the genus *Rhododendron* into units (43 of them, at present) of closely related species.

**Truss:** the flower cluster of rhododendrons.

**Variety:** a selected clone of a species (as opposed to 'cultivar' which refers to a *hybrid* plant).

## FOR MILD CLIMATES: MADDENII SERIES RHODODENODRONS

In coastal California gardens wherever winter temperatures rarely dip below 32° and where ocean moisture is a moderating summer influence, many of the exotic species and hybrids in the Maddenii series can be grown successfully out of doors. Hot, dry summers and freezing winters restrict them to cool greenhouses in other parts of the country.

Typically, these sorts produce either lily-like flowers or broad, saucer-shaped ones—always in white, often flushed pink or yellow. Fragrance is an outstanding asset possessed by nearly all species in the series and by many of their hybrids. Also characteristic—although not exhibited by *all* of these plants—is a rangy growth habit. A couple of years' pinching and pruning young plants can reward you with much more dense, shapely specimens than you would have if they were left to their own devices. With careful early guidance, Rhododendron 'Fragrantissimum', for example, can be trained into a hedge, a ground or bank cover, or an espalier on a wall or trellis. Many of these make fine container plants (with perfect drainage) because root systems are generally small.

Since many of these species are epiphytes in their native lands, this can be a guide to their particular requirements: perfectly-drained soil, and a moist (hence coastal) atmosphere.

*RHODODENDRON MADDENII.*

*RHODODENDRON FORMOSUM.*

*RHODODENDRON LINDLEYI.*

# How Rhododendrons and Azaleas Grow

## Native environments reveal basic cultural needs

Although the 900 or more rhododendron and azalea species are found growing in diverse natural situations—from alpine meadows to tropical rain forests, near sea level to 18,000 feet—their basic requirements for thrifty growth are the same everywhere. The diversity of plant forms in the genus reflects the variety of natural environments to which they have adapted.

Rather than restricting themselves to isolated locations with relatively similar climatic conditions, various rhododendron and azalea species have developed specialized features which enable them to extend their ranges into less-hospitable

ROCKY SLOPE where soil is shaded by small plants and fallen leaves helps duplicate a native environment.

climates while still insuring satisfaction of their basic needs. For example, needle-like foliage is found in some alpine species in order that the smallest possible leaf surface be exposed to the drying atmosphere, yet you will also find rhododendrons in the rainforest where leaf size can be vastly larger—to 3 feet long on *Rhododendron sinogrande*—because high humidity there prevents desiccation.

Although any generalization applied to rhododendrons and azaleas will bring forth at least one exception, it is safe to say that most species are natives of mountains or foothills. This statement alone holds the key to the five cardinal requirements of rhododendrons and azaleas:

1) Aerated soil (structure loose enough that air can enter spaces between particles as water drains out),
2) Acid soil (*pH* 4.5-6.0),
3) Cool, moist soil (but well-drained),
4) Shelter from wind and excessive sun,
5) Cool and humid atmosphere.

Mountainous situations imply more sloping land than level, and it is true that most rhododendrons and azaleas are hillside shrubs. Sloping land usually implies good drainage, as water seeks the lowest possible level; furthermore, there is a measurable decrease in temperature as you go higher into mountainous country. At the same time there is also an increase in rainfall: Warm moisture-laden clouds rise against mountainsides, cool, and condense moisture as they rise—producing rain. High rainfall and low temperatures promote the accumulation of all dead organic materials (leaves, branches) since the organisms that break down these materials are less active at lower temperatures. The result is a loose, largely organic "soil" in which rhododendrons and azaleas flourish. At the extreme adaptation to these conditions are the epiphytic species: rhododendrons which grow on

*SHELTERING TREES, water, and dense growth to shade the ground all contribute to the good health of R. occidentale. This Western native grows from southern Oregon to southern California.*

rocks, in the branches of trees or other rhododendrons, existing from whatever nutrients come with the rains or lodge in the mosses in which they have attached their roots.

Rhododendron and azalea roots have responded to these conditions in two fashions. First, they have become accustomed to a lightweight, porous, well-drained but moist rooting medium; this evolution has made them extremely sensitive to conditions in which they encounter either dry or "suffocated" soil. Second, because these soils are so loose, their roots have never needed the ability to penetrate heavy clay-like soils; consequently, all roots of this genus are fibrous and fine-textured, unable to extend into the dense soils found in many gardens.

Another feature associated with accumulation of organic material is increasing soil acidity. Leaves and other plant remains release organic acids as they decompose; wherever accumulation is faster than decomposition, an acid condition follows. Therefore: the higher the elevation the cooler the temperature; the cooler the temperature the more the rain; the more rain the more organic material accumulates; and, the more organic material accumulates the more acid will be the soil.

Notice the repeated mention of rainfall. This points out the dependence of rhododendrons and azaleas on abundant atmospheric moisture. Fortunately, this does not mean that you need to syringe their foliage every day that it doesn't rain: Many rhododendrons have developed a system of minute hairs or scales on the undersides of their leaves which retard excessive transpiration during dry periods yet allow for continual transpiration during prolonged rainy spells. It does mean, however, that a moist atmosphere measurably contributes to their good health by imposing less of a burden on the capillary system to replace moisture being lost through the leaves.

Whenever wild rhododendrons or azaleas are found growing in full sun or in exposed locations they are often the dominant—if not only—vegetation in that area. By their numbers and density they provide mutual protection from the dehydrating action of wind and sun. Only in numbers can they survive in such situations, and it is the exceptional species that do so. Ordinarily, they are forest plants, sometimes forming the dominant vegetation *beneath* broad-leafed or coniferous trees. In general, the smaller-leafed plants (often the smaller plants) can take more exposure because their leaves present less surface to the forces of dehydration.

# Success with Rhododendrons and Azaleas

## Careful preparation, planting are keys to healthy plants

The Pacific coast from Santa Cruz to Vancouver, the Appalachian Mountains, many parts of Great Britain, New Zealand, Japan, and—of course—the Monsoon regions of South-East Asia are "Rhododendron Country." Although rhododendrons and azaleas are also grown very successfully in many other regions, gardeners in these favored spots of the world can often grow them with less concern for basic cultural requirements, since nature has already provided congenial environments. However, even in relatively "foolproof" climates a little attention to the preferences of these plants will insure realization of their greatest potential.

Given an understanding of how rhododendrons and azaleas grow in their native habitats, you should be able to better accommodate them in your garden. Chances are you won't have the ideal wooded hillside with copious rainfall, but you can effectively simulate natural conditions by providing an environment which will satisfy the five cardinal requirements outlined in Chapter 2. Once again, these requirements are: 1) aerated soil, 2) acid soil, 3) cool, moist soil (but well-drained), 4) shelter from wind and too much sun, and 5) cool, humid atmosphere. Remember that each requirement is not a separate preference, to be satisfied

*WOODLAND SETTING provides a number of conditions favorable for success with rhododendrons and azaleas: continual mulch, dappled shade, and protection from full force of drying winds.*

in the order listed. By providing for only points 1-4 in your garden you cannot grow a rhododendron or azalea that will be four-fifths as good as one your neighbor grows by considering all five points. These are *interacting* requirements, mutually contributing to the plant's success; ignore one, and you diminish the effectiveness of your preparations to satisfy the other four.

## SITE SELECTION

Your first consideration in planting a rhododendron or azalea will be the choice of a suitable location in your garden. If you are aware of how sun, wind, air and water drainage, and other vegetation influence a site, you can locate plants where they will be the least subject to damaging climatic extremes. Not only will your plants be healthier and happier for this consideration, they will also require less attention than poorly-located specimens —ultimately a time-saver for the wise gardener.

### Sun Protection

The amount of sun a rhododendron or azalea can take without damage to the plant depends upon the ancestry of a hybrid or native habitat of a species, where you locate it in the garden, and in what area of the world you have your garden. Ideally, most of these plants should have as much sun as the foliage can stand without burning; sunlight promotes heavy flower production and compact growth, and properly matures the plant to resist winter cold damage. A few species and hybrids are especially sun-sensitive and require more shade than just short of being burned. Consult the individual descriptions (pages 68-78) for these.

How much shade you must provide for your rhododendrons or azaleas is directly related to the number of foggy, cloudy, or rainy days you can expect (on a yearly average) in your locality. The Pacific coast and much of Great Britain receive considerably more cloudy days during the growing season than the United States' eastern seaboard. Consequently, the Seattle gardener can get away with less shade for his plants than can the individual in Baltimore. Many gardeners in the fog-influenced areas from San Francisco north through coastal Oregon and Washington find they can grow most rhododendrons and azaleas in what would amount to full sun when the sun shines. The more days of sunshine you receive each year, the more shade you will have to consider.

RHODODENDRONS NEAR WATER can often take more exposure because of moisture content in the air.

In addition, the *angle* of the sun's rays determines the effect sunlight has on leaves: the greater the angle, the less intense is the sunlight and the more sun the plant can take. As latitude increases (on either side of the equator) so does the angle of the sun's rays; thus, rhododendrons in Boston gardens actually require more sunshine each day than do those in Baltimore.

Many of the tough hybrid rhododendrons popular in the eastern United States will perform well in full sun. This is, however, a matter of endurance rather than preference. Just as too much wind increases the transpiration rate—putting an added burden on the roots to supply leaves with water (to say nothing of the added burden on the gardener to supply it to the roots)—so does full sun. Unless you are growing one of these *catawbiense* hybrids, an alpine or small-leafed type, or deciduous azaleas you will find most larger-leafed species and hybrids must have some shade to avoid leaf burn.

## Wind Protection

In contrast to sun protection, shelter from wind can be prescribed categorically for all areas. Too much wind will increase transpiration rates to the point where roots can not supply additional water as fast as leaves are losing it. This is especially important in areas where soil freezes in winter: Rhododendrons and azaleas can not absorb moisture from frozen soil, with the result that winter winds can fatally dehydrate a plant.

Wind screens of other plants can provide attractive backgrounds for rhododendrons and azaleas in addition to serving as protection. Be sure that whatever you plant close to your rhododendrons or azaleas is deep-rooted or does not have invasive roots. A number of conifers are often favorite background subjects, especially those which are pyramidal to columnar and don't take up much garden space.

A good temporary wind protection (until background plants develop)—and a fine permanent solution, as well—is a lathhouse or a lath screen placed to shelter plants from the windward side. If you choose a lath screen (or "fence" of any material) to protect your plants, place it at a distance of about 3 times its height from the plants you want sheltered. Gardeners in all areas can profitably use the lath screen or house as a wind buffer; in addition, cold-climate gardeners will find it helpful as winter protection (pages 27-29).

If you are in doubt as to how much wind a particular rhododendron or azalea will tolerate, remember that the larger the leaves are, the more shelter the plant will need.

## Exposures

A northern exposure is the safest location for rhododendrons and azaleas. There, sun rarely strikes the plants, yet—if the location is *open* to the north—the amount of light received will be entirely satisfactory for good growth. A north-facing *slope* is even better: What sun strikes the leaves will be at an angle (and so less intense) while cold air will drain away from plants, minimizing winter injury.

Eastern exposures are generally successful everywhere, and particularly so where mornings are often overcast. In the eastern United States, however, early morning sun in winter can damage frozen leaves and flower buds of early-flowering sorts by thawing them too rapidly. If cold-climate gardeners provide some early morning shelter for the early ones, eastern exposures can be as satisfactory as northern.

A location facing west provides adequate sun and shade ratios; the problem here is afternoon heat. Rhododendrons backed by shrubs or trees may succeed where ones against a west-facing wall will burn.

Southern exposures are almost always too hot unless you live in a fog belt or can provide high overhead shade. South *slopes* can be made endurable for rhododendrons or azaleas if you mulch them well and water often, but the extra attention the plants require strongly suggests selection of a more congenial site.

Before selecting an exposure for your plants, be sure to check the direction of prevailing winds. The northern exposure that is buffeted by north winds loses much of its advantage until you provide some wind protection for rhododendrons or azaleas planted there (see "Wind Protection" on this page).

## Woodland Plantings

Rhododendrons and azaleas are, for the most part, woodland natives—whether the woodland be conifers, broad-leafed trees, or other rhododendrons. You can scarcely do better than give them an open wood (where treetops do not touch) with dappled sun. The shelter of trees minimizes summer high temperatures and winter lows by several degrees, while the changing patterns of sunlight on leaves eliminates the burning hazard. Because a canopy of trees reduces loss of soil warmth at night, a woodland location is especially good for hybrids or species which are susceptible to damage by freezing due to their early spring growth or late ripening of growth in fall.

The principal danger in woodland situations—especially as plantings age—is *too much* shade. Be sure you thin out the trees (if this is necessary) *before* you plant your rhododendrons or azaleas; attempts to remove trees from established plantings endanger the plants you are trying to benefit.

As a general rule, plant your rhododendrons and azaleas away from tree trunks unless trees are tall and open. If you can place your rhododendrons where they will have clear sky overhead they will benefit from all rainfall and still receive enough shade from adjacent trees as light patterns change during the day.

Mature oaks and many pines are first choices for woodland gardens. They generally are not surface rooted, so offer little competition for water and nutrients; the shade they provide is filtered, not dense; and their leaves and needles decompose slowly, providing a long-lasting acid mulch. Other non-competitive trees to associate with rhododendrons and azaleas are: deciduous magnolias, Liquidambar, Dogwood, Silver Bell trees (Halesia), Snow Bell trees (Styrax) and Sour Gum (*Nyssa sylvatica*).

Avoid planting your rhododendrons or azaleas under dense or surface-rooted trees. Among these unsuitable associates are: ash, beech, elm, maple, poplar, pin oak, and sycamore. Black walnuts and horse-chestnuts have leaves which become toxic as they decompose, while lindens, tulip trees, and some walnuts harbor insects which secrete a "honeydew" which may become a foothold for fungus diseases if it lands on rhododendron foliage and is not washed off.

Birch trees are both surface-rooted and a host for aphids which secrete a bothersome honeydew. Even so, birches provide a desirable sun filter and wind screen, and are attractive companions for rhododendrons and azaleas. You can safely plant *near* birch trees, but not under them.

City dwellers can take advantage of man-made forests of buildings which offer much the same sun and wind protection as do woodland trees.

## SOIL PREPARATION

The description of natural rhododendron soil on pages 14-15 holds the key to your understanding the importance of thorough soil preparation—and usually modification—before planting. A healthy plant can hardly be expected to develop from "unhappy" roots.

*Aeration* is the foremost requirement for successful rhododendron and azalea soil. This condition implies more than just a soil into which air can penetrate; such soils are also well-drained (so roots never drown in standing water) and are loose enough for fine roots to penetrate easily. With this aeration, however, must be a continually cool and moist (not wet) root environment; add this requirement to aeration and you get a soil that has to be largely organic—composed of vegetative remains in various stages of decomposition.

Organic materials, as they decompose into soil, go through a predictable life-cycle, different only in length from one material to another. Early stages remove nitrogen from the soil as the decomposing organisms use it to perform their tasks, while the materials release organic acids as they break down. The release of acids and uptake of nitrogen decrease as the cycle heads toward completion, and the end product has a neutral reaction.

The importance of this decomposition life-cycle to rhododendrons and azaleas is twofold. First, the organic material used to prepare the proper texture for the planting soil should be partially decomposed and slow to break down; such a material will not present serious competition for nitrogen and will maintain its structure long enough for the plants to establish themselves in a properly aerated soil. Second, a slowly decomposing material will preserve an acid soil environment at least until surface mulches begin breaking down enough to supplement the initial acidity.

The organic material which meets many of these requirements is peat moss: When you buy it, it has already undergone considerable decomposition but will last for a number of years before completely breaking down. Various grades and types are available, but you should look for a coarse-textured kind which will give you a looser, better-aerated soil structure than will a fine-textured peat. European sphagnum peat is usually a good choice as are many of the Canadian products. In the East and Pacific Northwest you may find locally-produced peat which will be entirely suitable.

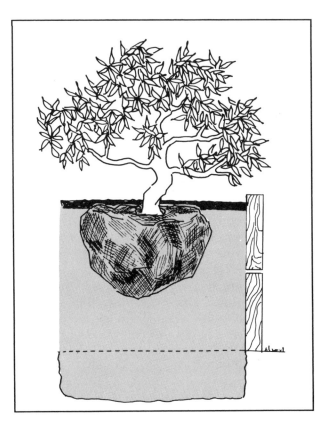

*RAISED BEDS 18 inches above soil grade are good where alkaline water, heavy soil are problems.*

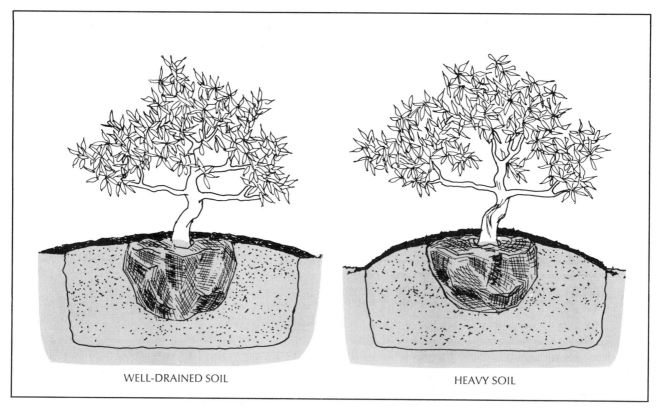

WELL-DRAINED SOIL HEAVY SOIL

*WHERE SOIL DRAINS WELL, rhododendrons and azaleas are planted in prepared soil with root crowns several inches above grade. In heavy soils they may be planted considerably higher and mulched well.*

Nevertheless, peat moss has its drawbacks, especially when it constitutes more than half the planting mix in raised beds or containers. Initially, you have to squeeze water into it (just *add* water and peat floats), and you must keep it moist thereafter; should it dry out, water will run off the peaty soil surface rather than penetrate. The clue to wetting peat then is to break the surface tension—do this by adding a small amount of a wetting agent to the water you pour onto the peat. Many commercial fertilizers now contain a "penetrator" to help overcome this water runoff problem; if you use such a fertilizer, be sure it is formulated for acid-loving plants.

Many other materials provide shorter-term benefits than does peat moss but will be as satisfactory *if* you follow a regular mulch and fertilizer program. Pine needles—fresh or rotted—work well as a soil additive, as do many by-products of regional agriculture such as spent hops, soy bean hulls, and grape or apple pomace. Oak litter (leaves, twigs, and decaying smaller branches) is also an excellent soil amendment wherever it is available. Ground bark is becoming increasingly popular as a substitute for peat moss.

Sawdust, as a soil amendment or as a mulch, remains a controversial item. Gardeners on the west coast—and especially in the Pacific Northwest where supplies are abundant—find it works well as a component of planting mixes if it is well aged or if additional nitrogen is supplied to help it decompose. Without the admixture of coarser organic materials, however, sawdust tends to create a soil too soggy for the best root environment; aged wood shavings or chips give you a looser soil texture. East coast rhododendron and azalea growers have had very mixed results from plantings in sawdust-conditioned soils. One risk they encounter is overstimulated plant growth as a result of trying to balance nitrogen removal; freezing winter weather then takes its toll on these plants. Many of these plantings have also had an unusual amount of trouble with Rhododendron Wilt. These two problems cause most easterners to avoid all sawdust unless it is *thoroughly* aged.

Partially-decomposed organic materials are preferable to raw materials at planting time because they require less nitrogen to complete their breakdown. If you use any undecomposed organic products then, be sure to include a partially-decomposed material (like leaf mold) in your preparation to supply additional organisms to help break them down. Very light applications of ammonium sulfate every month to six weeks during the growing season will help balance nitrogen taken from the soil by the decomposing matter. Eastern growers—and those in other cold-winter climates—should use extreme caution when applying ammonium sulfate; new out-of-season growth stimulated by excessive nitrogen is likely to be ruined by fall and winter freezes.

If you prepare your planting area a year or more before setting plants out, you can work into the soil almost any undecomposed organic material— even sawdust, if you also work in coarse-textured materials with it. By allowing the various materials a year in which to decompose in the soil before you plant your rhododendrons or azaleas, you avoid the risk of their robbing the plants of nitrogen needed for proper growth. Ammonium sulfate added to the soil will hasten the breakdown of raw organic materials—about 2 pounds to 100 square feet.

Since proper aeration and good drainage go hand in hand, you should determine what sort of drainage you have. Dig a hole 18 inches deep and fill it with water; if, within an hour, the water is gone, your soil's drainage is satisfactory.

Soil which is too sandy is easier to adjust for rhododendron culture than is heavy clay. With sand you are assured of good drainage: the problem is moisture retention, which can be achieved by the addition of organic matter. Heavy clay soils, on the other hand, are more difficult to adjust because the soil surrounding your prepared area will always drain more slowly; small planting holes can become catch basins for water, drowning rhododendron roots in short order. Planting rhododendrons and azaleas in raised beds or mounded areas of specially prepared soil will often be your best solution in heavy clay areas; this way, the rooting area above the grade of surrounding soil will never be saturated for prolonged periods. For best results, raised beds should extend about 18 inches above the soil grade. You should also incorporate into the top 2 feet of native clay soil materials to help improve its texture and drainage.

If you have only one or two plants to set out in heavy soil, you can generally achieve a satisfactory root environment if you excavate a hole 18 inches deep and 2 feet wide. Check to be sure drainage is satisfactory (see above); then discard this clay and refill the hole with a mixture of 40% organic material (at least half peat moss), 40% topsoil (not clay),

and 20% sand. Be sure that this prepared soil rises several inches above the surrounding grade level.

Because their root systems are not deep, rhododendrons and azaleas can be grown over an alkaline soil with relative safety. Raised beds or mounds are the most satisfactory planting situation in alkaline areas and are good insurance against alkalinity encroaching from surrounding soil. Even with raised plantings, however, prepare the top 12 inches of native soil beneath the plantings with organic materials to improve soil texture.

WIND SCREEN OF CONIFERS is practical, attractive. Upright types won't encroach on plantings.

## PLANTING A RHODODENDRON OR AZALEA

Rhododendrons ready-to-plant from the nursery will almost always be in cans or with the root ball wrapped in burlap. Azaleas may be received in either cans or ball-and-burlap, and also in pots, plant bands, or flats of rooted cuttings.

Regardless of how the plants have been prepared for sale, your first responsibility is to keep them moist until you can plant them. Meanwhile, in the prepared soil at the planting site, dig holes which will leave the juncture of roots and stem 2-3 inches above grade level of unprepared soil after planting is completed. In time your prepared soil will settle, and rhododendrons planted with root crowns at the grade level will eventually find themselves too low for satisfactory growth: Water will collect in this basin, soil will tend to wash in, and roots will be forced to grow upward to remain at the surface. High planting assures the roots their preferred surface position and that the plant will never become drowned or buried.

Before you set plants in their locations, remove the can, burlap, or other covering from the soil ball and *carefully* expose the root ends. If plants are in loose fibrous soil (as they should be), you can do this with your fingers; an alternate method is to *gently* wash away some soil with a garden hose. This action gives roots a chance to "reach out" and establish themselves in the soil you have prepared for your plants. Especially in heavy or ill-prepared soils rhododendrons and azaleas have been known to grow for a number of years without sending roots into surrounding soil; when nutrients and acidity are finally exhausted in the original root ball, these plants die.

If you have a plant which has been in its container so long that roots are dense and matted, you can encourage roots to extend into new soil by a careful root-pruning. With a *sharp* knife, cut away ½-inch of matted roots from the edges of the root ball of a 1-gallon plant—1 inch from plants in larger containers.

Newly planted rhododendrons and azaleas need to be firmly anchored but not forced into the soil. After you place them in their planting holes, fill in around root balls with prepared soil, lightly compacting it with your hands. Thoroughly water the soil replaced around the new plants; this will establish the best contact between root balls and surrounding soil. Never press a plant in with your foot on the root ball; the less the soil is compressed the better will be the aeration.

The point to remember with balled-and-burlapped plants, and with all plants after their removal from cans or pots, is that roots are very close to the surface of their root balls; for this reason you should see that root balls *never dry out*—even slightly—before the plant is planted.

### Transplanting A Rhododendron Or Azalea

A dense fibrous root system and a habit of shallow rooting make rhododendrons and azaleas among the easiest of shrubs to transplant. Even large old specimen rhododendrons may be moved, success virtually assured if the plant is in good health and reasonable care is exercised during the operation.

You could relocate a rhododendron or azalea at any time of year when it is not in active growth or the ground is not frozen. However, best results follow when you observe the timing proposed for planting new plants in the garden. Specimens in full bloom don't suffer from a move, but plants in bud may flower somewhat later than normal for the variety.

You can assume the plant's root-system extends out as far as its branches reach, but you can take a somewhat smaller root ball with safety. Figure your root ball should have a diameter equal to two-thirds the plant's height. First, with a spade, cut a circle of the calculated diameter and to the spade's depth around the plant to be moved. For larger plants, where the root ball might break if pressure were applied on one side by a spade, dig a trench around the plant and undercut the root system. Carefully raise the root ball just enough to insert a piece of partially rolled up burlap halfway under the plant; then, carefully raise the root ball from the opposite side enough to pull the rolled part out flat. Now, the entire root ball is resting on a burlap square. If you used a large enough piece of material you will be able to lift the corners of burlap over the top of the root ball, tie the opposite corners, and wrap the burlapped ball with twine. The plant is then ready to move.

Even for medium-sized plants which could be dug without the aid of burlap, it is good insurance to wrap the root system once the plant is removed from the earth. Any movement *could* break off part of the root ball, but a burlap wrapping prevents roots from being exposed, should this happen.

Remove burlap from the root ball when you plant your rhododendron or azalea. If the plant is so large that this would be difficult without possibly damaging the root system, cut away as much burlap as you can, exposing the sides of the root

# TRANSPLANTING A RHODODENDRON

*CUT CIRCLE around plant's drip line with spade; then dig trench around root ball and undercut it.*

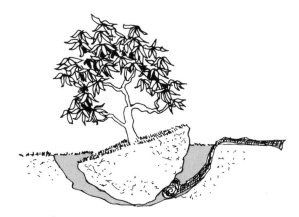

*TILT ROOT BALL away from you and place partly-unrolled burlap beneath, roll side up.*

*TILT PLANT BACK onto unrolled burlap, unroll remainder on other side; bring burlap up around root ball.*

*DETAIL OF BURLAPPING plant; wrap root ball with material, tie with twine. Move large plants on pallet.*

*PLACE PLANT in hole where soil has been prepared; root ball must be higher than surrounding grade.*

*REMOVE as much burlap as you can, then fill in around root ball with prepared soil. Water well and mulch.*

ball. Burlap remaining beneath the root ball will decay in time, but the majority of the roots will be free to extend into surrounding soil.

One word of caution: *never* lift anything but a small plant by its main stem when moving it from one place to another. The weight of roots and soil could cause damaging root breakage. You can move large heavy plants across a garden on a pallet or "skid" made from a sheet of plywood or lightweight metal; attach the ends of a rope to the 2 forward corners of the pallet so that you can pull the load easily.

### When To Plant

In the eastern United States—and in all areas which experience equally-severe winters—many growers prefer to plant or transplant rhododendrons and azaleas as early in the spring as is possible. This gives them the maximum amount of time to establish themselves before freezing weather arrives in fall. Fortunately, these areas usually have considerable summer rainfall—an aid to the gardener trying to keep plants moist during their first season. Those who prefer to plant later still do it in time to take advantage of maximum root development in August and September.

The Pacific Northwest (west of the Cascades), most of California, and parts of Great Britain have winter weather which poses less of a hazard to plant survival. Many locations within these milder-winter territories have hot summers and, in California, no summer rainfall. Here, rhododendrons and azaleas are better planted in late September through October so they may benefit from cool moist winters to become established. Then, when summer warmth arrives these plants will have a root system large enough to keep up with a high transpiration rate and will be less bothered by summer leaf burn than will plants set out in spring.

### MULCHES

A constant mulch is unquestionably a cornerstone to successful rhododendron and azalea culture. In the wild, these plants grow with a blanket of leaves over their roots; while the lower layer decomposes, a new supply is constantly falling to replace that which becomes "soil." As these leaves (or needles) break down, they create a loose, fibrous layer for the roots to grow up into; they release organic acids which help provide the acid condition necessary for maintaining proper nutrient availability; and the thickness of the layer keeps soil cool during the day, warmer than unmulched soil throughout the night, and conserves moisture.

Oak leaves and pine needles are first choices for

*ROCK MULCH simulates native conditions for many alpine species, is attractive throughout the year. Rounded stones look best as a mulch; be sure they are not of limestone origin.*

mulching rhododendrons and azaleas, although most hardwoods and conifers will provide satisfactory mulching material. Exceptions to this are maple leaves which form an air-tight mat and break down too rapidly, and leaves from trees grown on alkaline soils.

Sawdust and wood by-products other than bark —unless already rotted—may need additional nitrogen to supply the organisms which are breaking down the raw materials. These decomposing organisms can compete with plants for available nitrogen in the soil, causing a nitrogen deficiency in the plants if there's not enough nitrogen for both. A bushel of raw sawdust requires 1/2 pound ammonium sulfate to satisfy its nitrogen requirements; aged steer manure or sludge can be mixed with sawdust or wood chips in about equal parts to provide the necessary nitrogen with less danger of over-stimulating the plants. Here, again, the use of sawdust is shunned by most east coast growers but employed successfully by many in the west.

Peat moss, alone, is difficult to use as a mulch; if it dries, it forms a surface layer which is impervious to water. Even as a component of a mixed mulch it contributes little more than bulk, and it breaks down so slowly as to be of no use in maintaining a constant organic acid supply. Ground bark or bark chips (available in several sizes) are superior to peat moss as a mulch: attractive, very long-lasting, and no barrier to water penetration.

Mulches are a natural aid to weed control, and will also control the over-zealous gardener who might be tempted to cultivate under his rhododendron. This is always an injurious practice, destroying the surface network of roots. Any weeds that appear in your plantings should be *pulled by hand*.

Materials, like sawdust, which pack down should be used no more than 2 inches thick so that roots won't be smothered; pine needles, oak leaves, ground sugar cane, and other loose mulches which allow air to reach the soil surface can be applied in thicker layers.

You can apply a mulch at any time of year and should do so whenever one is not present. Since deciduous trees drop their leaves in fall, this would seem to be a "natural" time to apply mulches and is preferred in areas of winter snowfall. There, a renewed mulch in autumn will also serve as winter protection and could be so thick as to reach the lowest leaves on a rhododendron or azalea plant. By springtime this mulch will have

been reduced down to about half its autumn depth; any excess should be raked off to avoid smothering plants. Gardeners in warmer climates —especially where summers are dry and hot— should be very sure that plants are mulched at the onset of warm weather.

Periodically check your mulch to be certain it still covers the root zone. Larger birds and squirrels can scratch away enough mulch to expose delicate feeding roots to the drying air.

## FERTILIZING

Many gardeners regard fertilizers and fertilization as a cure for all plant problems, and the first and last resort for making a sick plant well and a healthy plant healthier. However, plants—unlike animals—manufacture some of their own foods and therefore do not need to be *constantly* supplied and re-supplied. The popular use of the term "plant food" for fertilizer only helps perpetuate the misconception of plants as hungry, dependent "children."

### Why Fertilize?

Because soils do not supply dependably enough of the essential nutrients plants need to synthesize their chlorophyll for manufacturing carbohydrates, fertilizers are needed to provide supplementary nutrients for better growth. An intelligent fertilization program is based upon knowledge of what nutrients are needed for overall plant health, the times of year plants may need them, and when *not* to fertilize. Rhododendrons in particular are not heavy feeders; if your plants are flowering well and are producing satisfactory, healthy new growth each year (6-8 inches for the larger-leafed kinds, less for smaller ones), you probably don't need to help them along. At the most they would need only a light application of a complete acid fertilizer. Rhododendrons and azaleas will, however, give you a gratifying response to fertilizers— especially nitrogen (see next page). This is an advantage to the commercial grower who is concerned with producing salable plants in the least amount of time. Home gardeners, on the other hand, may discover that their over-fertilized plants rather quickly outgrow their intended garden spots.

### What To Use And When To Use It

Nitrogen speeds vegetative growth and gives rich green leaf color; phosphorus promotes root activity, ripening and maturing of plant tissues, and

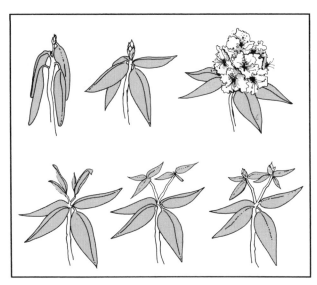

*RHODODENDRON'S YEAR of growth: winter wilt through spring flowers to new growth and buds.*

is necessary for production of flowers and fruit; potassium encourages development of plant tissues, the manufacture and movement of sugars and starches within the plant.

The greatest need for nitrogen is when plants are beginning to make active growth and during the growth period. Outdoors, these growth periods are triggered by the proper temperature-moisture combination—for most plants, spring, when weather warms and moisture is plentiful.

Nitrogen, applied at other times of year when weather is as warm or warmer than early spring, will trigger more new growth if moisture is also provided. Greenhouse growers appreciate this response, as they can produce large plants more rapidly in their controlled environment than would be possible outdoors. Most gardeners, however, will find their rhododendrons and azaleas at a disadvantage if stimulated into later growth. Summer temperatures increase transpiration rates, and young growth wilts easily unless additional water is supplied; this same late growth often has insufficient time (and that under trying conditions) to properly mature before cool autumn weather comes along. Where frosts or freezing winters are common, these unripened plants are likely to be damaged or killed.

Since rhododendrons and azaleas initiate new growth immediately following bloom (or during it, for some varieties), this is the season when they may need additional nitrogen. At this time you have a choice of several approaches to nutrient application. You can apply a "complete" acid fertilizer just as buds swell, and repeat applications monthly until new growth gets underway in later spring; or your first application could be of ammonium sulfate followed up by a complete fertilizer at similar intervals. In severe winter country, you should withhold nitrogen by mid-June, although phosphorus and potassium may be applied later than that to help mature the season's growth. These two nutrients are generally available combined in equal proportions in a formula without nitrogen (such as 0-10-10).

Another possible approach is to supply the necessary nutrients separately rather than in a complete package. One San Francisco area grower has good success with ammonium phosphate right after bloom, giving a second application to plants that don't respond within three weeks. A month after the ammonium phosphate application, he begins the first in a series of monthly applications of a phosphorus-potassium fertilizer in a commercial formulation which contains these nutrients in equal amounts. His cutoff time for this is Thanksgiving—or during August for colder climates. With both fertilizers—ammonium phosphate and the phosphorus-potassium formulation—the plants receive a tablespoon for each foot of height, scattered underneath the plants and thoroughly drenched in. With a "separate" approach like this, you might need to give your plantings a periodic renewal of trace elements.

Complete fertilizers *especially formulated for acid-loving* plants are a good choice for an inorganic source of balanced nutrients. Avoid using ordinary complete fertilizers as they may contain nitrogen in a form that will leave an alkaline residue in the soil or will promote intake of basic elements. Only nitrogen in an ammonium form should be used. Ammonium sulfate is a favorite inorganic source of nitrogen alone for many rhododendron and azalea growers because it becomes rapidly available to plants and leaves an acid residue.

Organic nitrogen sources, including cottonseed meal, fish meal, tankage, and fertilizers containing urea formaldehyde (U.F.), release nitrogen more slowly than the inorganic fertilizers and so minimize the risk of burning plants; organics provide a weaker stimulus but remain effective over a longer period.

Use any of these fertilizers (especially the inorganics) only in the quantities recommended on their packages—or even less. Small and young plants in particular are often sensitive to excessive amounts of fertilizers; when in doubt, use a *light* hand. Apply all fertilizers directly on top of your mulch and water in thoroughly.

## Liquid Fertilizers

Liquid fertilizers can be utilized immediately, as opposed to granulated sorts which may not take effect for a week or more and may be available to the plants longer than you wished. For these reasons, you can use liquid fertilizers later in the season than dry kinds you apply to the soil. With these fertilizers you also have much closer control over the *quantity* of fertilizer your plant receives; if you use the proper dilution for the particular fertilizer, you avoid most risk of burning your plants with excessive amounts.

Providing nutrients that rhododendrons and azaleas can absorb through their leaves is especially beneficial in certain cases. Some broad-leafed types and the epiphytic species or their hybrids are accustomed to receiving some percentage of nutrients through their leaves, although nature rarely provides the carefully balanced formulations and optimum strengths that commercial foliar fertilizers do. You can also measurably increase growth of seedling plants with a regular foliar program; applications can be as often as every two weeks until mid-summer. Sorts with waxy, slick leaves will benefit the least from nutrients applied in this manner.

Evenings, *early* mornings, or other humid periods with little or no strong or direct sun are the best times for spraying foliar fertilizers. On sunny days, leaves are applying all their defenses against excessive transpiration, but in the cool dampness of mornings, evenings or cloudy days they are much more receptive to intake of moisture. Then, you also avoid burning leaves, which is possible if sunlight strikes water droplets from the spray. Gardeners in moist or humid areas often prefer to spray in early morning rather than late in the day. In these climates wet foliage at night may encourage fungus diseases. A "spreader" of a teaspoon of detergent to each gallon of solution gives good surface coverage, but in humid climates use a sticking agent with caution: Some growers feel this provides a foothold for fungus growth.

## WINTER PROTECTION

You can minimize your autumn garden chores if you understand the factors which affect a plant's hardiness. Some varieties may always be tender in your garden unless somehow protected, but those of marginal hardiness can be located and cared for in a manner to increase their adaptation to your climate and thereby reduce your care for them over winter. Even notably hardy specimens will benefit from your gardening savvy in exceptionally cold years.

In essence, you want to give your rhododendrons and azaleas a winter environment in which the temperature fluctuations will be: first, more gradual than in an exposed area and, second, less extreme. Probably more plants are lost (in a "normal" season) by their unsuccessfully trying to adjust to fast temperature changes than are lost as a result of low temperature alone. Water is expelled from plant cells into inter-cellular spaces as temperature falls; this water then freezes. However, when a plant is suddenly exposed to a rise in temperature it begins transpiring, but the cells are not able to regain water fast enough to supply their demands. The result is a wilted leaf, followed in time by a desiccated plant.

*NEARBY TREES AND SHRUBS moderate winter temperatures, discourage formation of late-season growth.*

## Preventive Measures

How do you provide protection from fast temperature changes? You might cover or shelter all your rhododendrons and azaleas, but since this involves the greatest possible amount of work, let's examine some preventive measures first.

Before you plant your rhododendron or azalea, carefully analyze the exposure of the planting site. Your problems will be increased if you select a position which encourages late fall and early spring growth. Planted against south walls, rhododendrons and azaleas will be tempted to grow during more of the year than plants located facing north. In northern exposures, greater shade or less direct light slows growth earlier in fall and shields plants from premature springtime. Similarly, plants growing under a canopy of trees or in partial shade of other plants will enter dormancy earlier than individuals in the open garden and will respond later to spring warmth.

Where early morning sun strikes frozen leaves and flower buds, damage will be more severe than in locations where air temperature rises gradually. For this reason, unsheltered eastern and southern exposures for early-flowering sorts are less desirable than north or west in the eastern United States and other cold-winter areas where sunny winter mornings outnumber cloudy ones.

Any warm sunny spot or a location open to frequent winds will accelerate water loss from plant tissues; if soil freezes through the root zone, there is no way for plants to re-supply the lost moisture. Wind protection can be supplied by topography, buildings or fences, or other plantings.

Mulches moderate temperature extremes in two ways. They maintain a more constant soil temperature than you would find in unmulched areas, and a mulch can prevent the ground from freezing to any great depth. Consequently, a mulched plant may find its lower roots in unfrozen soil; these roots can supply moisture to transpiring leaves.

Finally, never plant rhododendrons or azaleas in the lowest part of the garden—especially if this is a flat or "hollow" area with no further air drainage. Since cold air—like water—seeks the lowest possible level, your lowest garden spots will be the most subject to damage from freezing.

## Summer Care ... Where Soil Freezes In Winter

One cardinal rule of rhododendron and azalea culture is to keep the root zone moist (not wet) and cool. It may come as a surprise, then, to be told to taper off on water in August, but this is a technique which some growers in areas of frozen winter soils apply in order to better prepare plants for winter cold. If combined with a fertilizing schedule which will not promote late season growth, the water-deficit routine will slow the plants' growth and increase a buildup of sugars in their cells. These cells will then withstand freezing temperatures better than those rich in water and low in sugars.

The water-deficit process works like this: As a plant draws water from the soil, the upper half of the root zone dries out first because more roots are working there. When the upper roots exhaust the moisture available to them, the plant becomes dependent upon the fewer lower roots. With the decrease in number of water-supplying roots, the plant approaches a point where the water supply wavers between being adequate and inadequate. On cool days the leaves remain turgid but wilt on hot days. Or, the water supply may be just enough to keep the leaves from wilting except in the hottest hour of a warm August day. This water-deficit slows the growth processes; a plant at the wilting point functions fewer hours per day than does a plant with a water supply adequate for any emergency.

New leaves which droop during the day but return to their normal freshness in evening tell you the plant still has enough moisture in reserve; should they remain limp you know it's time to add more water. Rhododendron growers where summers are cool or moist (but where winters are freezing) often give their plants an early evening foliage spray to perk up drooping leaves. Gardeners in hot-summer climates where leaf-burn is a summer problem may employ a morning or evening foliage spray routinely so that leaves will *not* wilt during the day: Wilted leaves burn more readily than do those with enough moisture to remain turgid. Whenever foliage sprays become inadequate to prevent new leaves from wilting, plants are watered thoroughly so that moisture is sure to reach the lowest roots. Following this, the foliage spray is resumed.

Early August is the usual time to begin tapering off on water. By the time you can expect the first fall frosts, nights will have cooled enough that danger of growth stimulation is past; you can then resume normal watering. Be especially sure that your rhododendrons and azaleas are well-watered before soil freezes for winter. During that period the plants depend upon whatever moisture is in their tissues—roots can not extract any more water from frozen soil.

Two other aspects of good rhododendron and azalea culture, if observed, promote the success of a water-deficit program. Soil prepared to a depth of about 2 feet insures the existence of lower roots on which the thirsty plant can depend when surface roots no longer can supply water. A mulch over the planting area will maintain a cool root zone and minimize water loss from evaporation.

**Caution: New Plants.** The exception to the water-deficit treatment is newly-planted specimens: you may have to water these regularly during their first season, as their root systems won't be established enough to withstand an enforced drought. These plants will usually be small enough that you can easily provide shelter for them during their first winters.

**Words To Live By...**

Your greatest aid to winter protection—assuming your plants are properly situated—will be a growth cycle adjusted to your climate. Fertilize in spring to promote new growth, then go easy on the water in August and September to harden off growth. This timing determines, to a large degree, the ruggedness of your plants.

**Protective Devices**

The theory behind physical protection of plants during winter is the same as that discussed under proper site selection for cold climates: these crates, frames, and screens all serve to minimize the rapidity of temperature fluctuations. If you exercised care in locating your rhododendrons and azaleas, these measures may be necessary only for the first few years with possibly-tender sorts until the plants are definitely established. If, however, you have inherited plants which are unwisely placed for winter survival and it is too late to move them, employment of these protective devices could save your plants until spring when you can relocate them.

In areas of cold winters and also of hot, unfriendly summers (regardless of winter temperatures), lathhouses may provide enough protection for gardeners to grow varieties otherwise sensitive to their climates. Rhododendrons and azaleas too tender for exposed sites often are grown successfully in lathhouses. These can provide ample shelter during cold winters—even when the plants are planted in the ground. Certainly in areas with hot or dry summers the protection from sun and wind provided by a lathhouse reduces transpiration rates significantly, to the great benefit of the plants. Experimenters in the midwest and in central California have found lathhouses to be especially helpful. Probably the improved summer growth under lath better prepares the plants for withstanding winter severities.

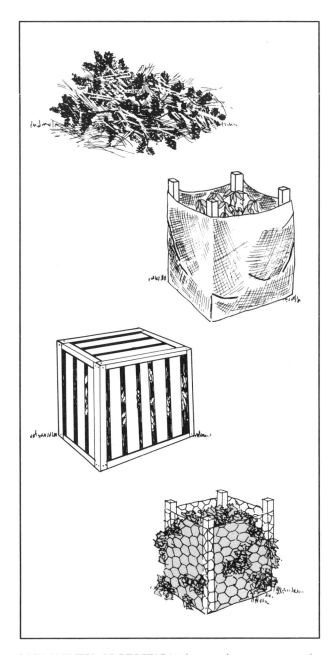

EASY WINTER PROTECTION for tender sorts: conifer branches arched over plant; burlap surrounding (but not touching) shrub; "lathhouse" made from crate; chicken-wire cage to hold insulating oak leaves.

## ALKALINE WATER AND SOIL

Gardeners in arid and semi-arid regions—especially in the southwest from Texas to California and east of the Cascades in the northwest—face a special and continual natural handicap to rhododendron and azalea culture: the alkaline salts in water and soils are hostile to all acid-loving plants. Fortunately, an analysis of the problem discloses solutions for it. The answer is constant vigilance—not a daily or even weekly routine, but seasonal treatment plus a sharp eye for danger signals.

Three things make the soil alkalinity problem acute in arid western areas:

**1. Soils are alkaline** in most low-rainfall areas, containing calcium and magnesium salts in varying degrees. Calcium salts produce $pH$ readings up to 8.5. (The $pH$ symbol expresses relative acidity or alkalinity. A $pH$ of 7 is neutral, readings below 7 are increasingly acid, above 7 are increasingly alkaline.)

Alkaline soils of the western United States differ in their types of alkalinity. In some soils it is sodium, not calcium, which plays the dominant role. A high concentration of sodium, in proportion to calcium, is far more toxic to plants than a calcium concentration; and, in addition, sodium binds itself to clay particles, affecting the degree of soil permeability. High-sodium soils, often called "black alkali" soils, are characterized by drainage which isn't just poor, it's almost nil.

**2. Domestic water is alkaline** in most of these low-rainfall areas and carries dissolved salts of calcium, magnesium, sodium, or other elements in varying amounts. Some fortunate southwest communities are served with water from wells or mountain reservoirs which is almost salt free, but most municipal supplies are more or less alkaline. Soil salinity resulting from irrigation water accumulating soluble salts in the upper layers of soil is a familiar problem to commercial growers, particularly those working with plants that gardeners know as "acid-loving," scientists as "sodium-sensitive."

**3. Summers are long and dry.** Not all gardeners in the southwest or east of the Cascades are conscious of the radical difference in watering procedures between these regions and the East. There, rains can do up to 90 per cent of summer watering, with the result that the soil is regularly leached with slightly acid water. Since their soils tend to be acid, eastern gardeners face an opposite soil problem: rain-leaching will lower the concentration of calcium salts to the point where there's actually a calcium shortage and "liming" is regularly practiced to replenish it.

In most sections of the southwest and east of the Cascades, on the other hand, there is a minimum of rain-leaching—up to 90 per cent of irrigation is artificial. Constant irrigation of upper soil layers already high in calcium with calcium-laden water makes concentrations even higher, and percentages of other salts rise along with them. Irrigation with softened waters, high in sodium rather than calcium, can create even more complications: $pH$ may go considerably higher (to 9.5), sodium concentrations can produce problems in soil permeability in time, and toxic symptoms may appear in many plants.

### Symptoms of Trouble

Here are four "danger signals" which demand attention if you are to maintain the good health of your rhododendrons and azaleas.

**1. Chlorosis.** Old mature leaves turn yellow, except for green lines along the leaf veins: High alkalinity reduces availability of iron and manganese. Both untreated (calcium) waters and softened (sodium) waters can bring this about though sodium's effects are usually more severe. The more alkaline the native soil is, the quicker an irrigation with saline waters will produce chlorosis. Texture and structure of soil is also important: Well-drained, sandy soils are less likely to become alkaline from saline water as quickly as will those higher in clay; and soils high in humus and soil bacteria have a stronger acid potential to work against many alkaline influences.

**2. Growth depression.** Experiments have shown definite depression of growth in some azaleas after prolonged irrigation with softened (sodium) water. Plants were stockier and bushier than those grown with water low in sodium.

**3. Salt injury or "burn"** is usually easy to identify by browned, burned tips and margins of leaves. Marked injury to some azaleas has been observed after a single season of overhead sprinkling even with waters of *low* salinity. Damage was more severe in plants watered by sprinkling than those which were flood irrigated, indicating that some salts were absorbed through the leaves. Salt concentrations can accumulate much more quickly in container plants than those grown in open ground, and injury shows up more quickly.

**4. Reduced soil permeability** is a long-term effect of continuous irrigation with softened (sodium) waters. This is essentially a reverse version of the softening process: Ions of sodium in the water replace ions of calcium in the soil, adhering to clay particles. After several seasons, sodium concentrations can bind soil particles together, breaking down soil texture and seriously reducing permeability.

## Corrective Action You Can Take

Ordinary garden watering may wet soil to a depth of a foot or so. Part of the water is absorbed by plant roots, the rest evaporates from the soil surface. Result: the salts are left as residue in the upper foot of soil. Each such irrigation adds an equal amount of residue. It's obvious, then, how quickly even weekly waterings may possibly bring salt concentrations up to harmful levels.

**1. Leaching** is more than irrigation: it is a deliberate flooding for several hours at a stretch. Even though the water used in flooding contains small amounts of dissolved salts, it will pick up salts which are present in higher concentrations—resulting from months of regular watering in the upper foot of soil—and carry them down into the lower soil levels, below reach of plant roots. In some cases a single heavy leaching in midsummer plus normal leaching action of winter rains is sufficient for virtually all subjects in the ground, but container plants may require it more often.

Leaching, of course, demands good drainage; the salts must be carried into lower levels of soil fairly easily. If you don't have good drainage, there isn't much you can do until you provide it.

This attack on salinity also involves fertility problems, since leaching will carry off soluble plant nutrients along with the salts. Soluble inorganic fertilizers, such as ammonium sulfate, will pass down into lower levels quite rapidly. If leaching is to be practiced, you can do either of these things to maintain soil fertility: Feed plants with a mild application of soluble fertilizer, liquid or dry, *after* leaching; or, use the insoluble, slow-acting organic fertilizers in a regular feeding program. Organic materials (like cottonseed meal) become fertilizers only after soil bacteria produce decomposition, which creates soluble materials available to the plant. Such soluble substances in the soil at time of leaching will drain off along with salts, but the raw material remains in the soil as organic humus for further action by soil bacteria.

**2. Add soil correctives.** You can usually determine which conditioner to use by observing performance of plants, condition of soil, and knowing what kind of tap water you have. Gardeners using softened water will generally turn to gypsum as a conditioner; those using unsoftened water, to sulfur.

*Soil sulfur* is most effective on high-calcium, alkaline soil, usually a result of prolonged irrigation with untreated calcium waters. Broadcast the sulfur (one pound per 100 square feet lowers pH one-half point) in early spring, just before weather warms up; sulfur is less active when temperatures are low. Warmth and moisture produce bacterial activity which slowly breaks sulfur down, producing sulfuric acid. The sulfuric acid reacts with insoluble calcium carbonate and bicarbonate in the soil to produce calcium sulfate (or gypsum) which is soluble and can be carried down into lower soil layers, out of reach of plant roots. A single spring application of sulfur is usually sufficient for a year.

The net effect of sulfur, then, is to lower the concentration of calcium carbonate in the soil. If calcium is not present in the soil to any degree, sulfur's action is simply to increase soil acidity.

*Gypsum,* or *calcium sulfate,* is indicated where sodium is the problem, mainly in borderline alkali areas or in districts receiving treated softened (sodium) water. Gypsum contains both sulfur and calcium; applied to the soil surface prior to leaching, calcium ions from gypsum reverse the process produced by sodium water. They replace sodium ions on soil particles, and sodium is carried off as soluble sulfate.

Gypsum applications on sodium soils make pronounced, prompt effects. Calcium causes flocculation — grouping of particles into small grains with air spaces between. Soil becomes more workable, more favorable for root growth.

Applying gypsum indiscriminately to soil won't harm most plants since very few species are affected by even saturated solutions of gypsum; it's one of the safest soil conditioners you can use. However, using gypsum on a soil in which trouble lies in an oversupply of calcium carbonates and bicarbonates will only increase concentrations of calcium beyond required levels. It won't remove the carbonate and bicarbonate ions which cause alkalinity; sulfur lowers the pH infinitely better.

You can use gypsum and sulfur together where the object is twofold; to lower concentrations of sodium (with gypsum), and to increase acidity for rhododendrons and azaleas (with sulfur).

# Troubleshooting Insects and Disease Problems

## Good culture is your best defense against plant problems

Although most favorite garden ornamentals have insect and disease enemies which occasionally threaten their beauty and health, rhododendrons and azaleas can be listed among the most trouble-free. True, there are a number of pests and infections which *can* use these plants as hosts, but only a very few are regarded as potentially serious problems and some of these appear only in specific regions of the country.

*TO "DEADHEAD" A RHODODENDRON after flowering, remove old bloom truss just below lowest flower.*

From the list of possible ailments, many can be traced to poor culture; heed the advice on pages 37 to 39 and you can thwart potential infirmities which only the careless grower will experience. A number of so-called "diseases" are rare, or are really not injurious to the plant; others occur only in the greenhouse where air is saturated and still.

The charts at the end of the chapter outline pests and diseases—their symptoms, controls, cautions, and relative importance. Following these you will find descriptions of injuries that can be caused by weather and by soil problems.

### SPRAYING HINTS

The most efficient spray coverage is possible only when the air is still. Mornings and evenings are usually periods of least air movement. Direct sunlight on spray droplets can become so intense as to severely burn leaves that are supposed to benefit from the spray. Here again, mornings and evenings (and, in addition, overcast days) are the best times for you to spray.

The waxy rhododendron leaves tend to repel rather than attract sprays; for the best coverage you will want to use a spreader in your spray solution. A household detergent is quite satisfactory. Inclusion of a sticking agent is, however, a somewhat controversial matter: some growers use it with no ill effects, while others claim it affords a foothold for fungus organisims. This will be of more concern if you spray during humid weather.

**Caution:** Some sprays should not be used during hot weather; these temperature restrictions should be noted on the spray container. Read all labels carefully to see if there are any limitations to a spray's use.

## CHLORINATED HYDROCARBONS

Great strides have been made in pest control during this century, no small part of it the result of war efforts to create sanitary environments in less-developed areas occupied by troops. The most famous (and one of the most effective) of these insect killers was DDT—one of a group of compounds known as chlorinated hydrocarbons, a term descriptive of their chemical makeup. In addition to DDT, most gardeners will recognize such familiar names as chlordane, lindane, and dieldrin in the list of chlorinated hydrocarbons.

One of the characteristics of this group of chemical compounds—in addition to initial effectiveness—is their residual behavior: Applications, in many cases, maintain their potency for several years while the chemicals themselves do not break down into less-toxic compounds. Unfortunately, this is also the characteristic which is causing chlorinated hydrocarbons to be regarded with increasing disfavor, to the point that some states have outlawed their use. Where they have been employed repeatedly in large-scale crop operations, their residue has contaminated the water and food supplies of wildlife. Birds and lower animals have not been killed outright, but the reproductive systems of some have been adversely affected, creating populations of infertile creatures. Although man and his pets are not known to suffer from a buildup of these compounds in body tissues, the damage incurred by us may be indirect—in the form of a gradually poisoned, unbalanced ecology.

The efficiency of chlorinated hydrocarbon compounds is not questioned, but much current chemical research is devoted to formulation of other insecticides which will minimize the health risk to other organisms. As a result, the recommendations for insect control in this chapter include none of the chlorinated hydrocarbons.

## CHLOROSIS

Soil acidity is measured in *p*H units, which represent hydrogen-ion concentrations. A *p*H of 7 is neutral—neither acid nor alkaline; readings above 7 are alkaline, below 7 are acid. The degree of alkalinity/acidity increases or decreases by ten times the previous level for each whole-number change. Thus, *p*H 8 is ten times more alkaline than *p*H 7 and is 100 times more alkaline than *p*H 6.

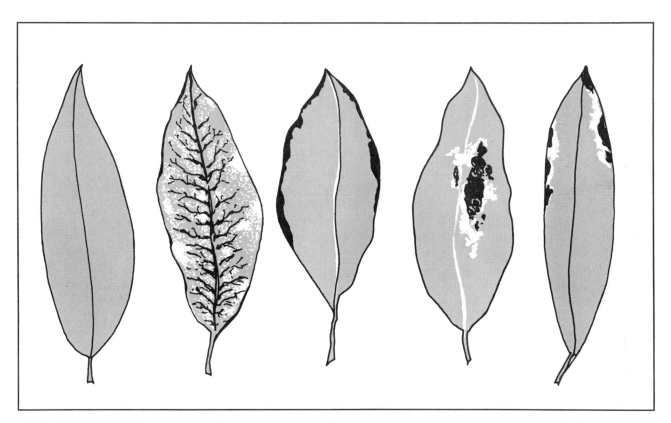

*FOUR LEAF TROUBLES. Left, normal leaf; dark veins on light leaf show chlorosis; brown margins indicate salts injury; sunburn shown by brown patches near center in winter, on edges in summer.*

Ordinarily rhododendrons and azaleas prosper in soils between pH 4 and 6. Recent research has disclosed, however, that acid soil is not always directly responsible for the good health of these plants: the acidity of the plants' *cell sap* is the critical factor. Internal acidity guarantees availability of iron within the plants' tissues; iron is essential to the production of chlorophyll which in turn manufactures carbohydrates in the leaves and is responsible for the green color. If iron is unavailable to the plant tissues, chlorosis develops; leaf veins remain green while the leaf turns yellow to white. This condition is not unlike anemia in humans and, unless corrected, can be fatal.

Loss of internal acidity can come about in several ways. The most common cause, of course, is alkaline soil—which may also be augmented by alkaline water. For a discussion of this problem and how you can combat it, see pages 30-31.

Another possible cause of chlorosis is an inability of the roots to absorb enough iron for the plant's needs. If you plant rhododendrons or azaleas too deep, their roots are unable to function efficiently until they are brought to the surface—

either by growing new roots in that direction or by your raising the plant. Meanwhile, the plant's health suffers.

Overwatering and overfertilization can kill enough roots that the remainder supply inadequate amounts of iron for the amount of top growth. Destruction of roots with the same consequences can also be accomplished by various weevil larvae, centipedes, or nematodes.

**What To Do For A Chlorotic Plant**

Applications of chelated iron in a foliage spray will tell you within a week or two whether the chlorosis resulted from a lack of available iron in the plant's cell sap. Within that time, the iron-deficient leaves will begin to show green spots which become increasingly larger until—in five to six weeks—the leaves will be entirely green again.

Although iron chelates in a foliage spray or in soil applications will provide iron in solution within the plant for as long as you wish to use it, you will generally be doing your plants more of a favor if you determine the cause of the chlorosis and apply the appropriate remedy. Especially in areas of alkaline soil, other elements are likely to become unavailable as the pH increases, requiring remedies in addition to iron chelates.

Chlorotic symptoms can also reflect the lack of elements other than iron. Magnesium deficiency can be determined by spraying the foliage with magnesium sulfate (Epsom Salts)—2 tablespoons per gallon of water. If leaves regain their green color, you can obtain a longer-lasting remedy by broadcasting magnesium sulfate crystals on the soil at the rate of 1 pound for each 100 square feet.

If a foliage spray of iron chelates or magnesium sulfate fails to bring about a shift back toward green, you might apply fritted trace elements (FTE) to the soil. These elements are released slowly but over a long period and can be valuable where chlorosis is not the result of a damaged root system.

Whenever chlorosis persists despite your efforts to overcome it and where there is no evidence of root damage, have your soil analyzed.

### SUN BURN

Damage from sun exposure appears as brown patches on leaves—round spots along edges and tips from summer sun, but elongated patches on either side of the mid-vein when winter sun is intense and soil is frozen. Rarely of major importance in themselves, the damaged spots offer a foothold

*PLANTS TOLERATE hot, dry summers better if humidity is raised by a daily overhead misting of water.*

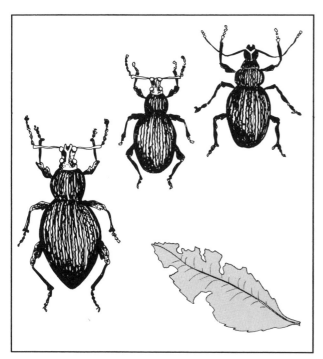

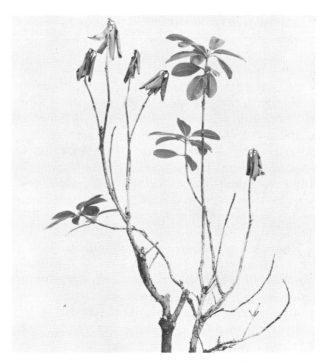

*THREE ROOT WEEVILS* (Brachyrhinus) *and their injury to leaves. Greatest damage is to roots and trunks.*

*RHODODENDRON WILT* (Phytophthora) *shows as browning wilted leaves. Disease first attacks the roots.*

for secondary fungus infections which can weaken the plant.

Any sun burn is the result of transpiration proceeding faster than the roots can resupply leaves with water. Your first line of defense is to see that plants have adequate moisture for their locations. Especially if your soil is likely to freeze during winter, be sure your plants are well-supplied with water just before freezing weather arrives.

Although rhododendrons and azaleas require plenty of *light* for best performance, too much sun works against them; remember that the larger the leaves, the less direct sun the plant needs. If you determine that your plants are poorly located, you would be wise to provide more sun shelter or move them.

Three other variable factors influence a plant's sun tolerance. Situations near water (or within a few miles of large water bodies) generally have enough moisture in the air that a given rhododendron or azalea can take more direct sun than it can in a drier atmosphere. The age of a plant and how long it has been established in its location influence its sensitivity to all conditions; young and newly-planted specimens are more subject to damage than are older and established plants. Then, aside from the leaf-size rule-of-thumb, some varieties are inherently susceptible to sun burn.

## SALTS INJURY; WIND BURN

These two problems, arising from different causes and requiring different treatments, are nevertheless similar in the appearance of their damage. In order to determine which is affecting your plants, look at which growth is injured: Browned margins and tips on older leaves indicate salts damage; new growth with browned edges has wind burn.

The remedy for wind burn is fairly simple: give your plants some protection until you have a chance to move them to a more congenial location. The salinity problem and its solutions are discussed on pages 30-31

## FROST DAMAGE AND WINTER INJURY

This is one of the recurring problems that gardeners in cold-winter climates learn to live with. Winters, themselves, you can anticipate, and provide suitable protection for tender plants. It is the unusually early fall frosts or the unexpected late spring ones that do the damage.

Frost injury assumes several forms, depending upon severity. Leaves may look distorted and rough or they may be killed outright; sometimes, after spring frosts, new growth will be killed on leaf tips and edges while leaf bases and new stems remain undamaged because new leaves fold over one another in scale fashion, protecting the bases of those higher on the stem.

If a particular plant is consistently injured by frost each year, it is too tender for the site in which it is growing and possibly for your part of the country. Move it to a more sheltered place in your garden, avoiding low spots with no air drainage which become frost pockets in cold weather.

Injury from winter low temperatures is easily recognizable as flower buds are killed and turn brown or when watery blisters appear along leaf margins. This damage affects but little the overall health of your rhododendrons and azaleas; it is the less-noticeable injury which can be fatal.

Freezing temperatures are especially dangerous to unprotected branches and main stems, causing the bark to split and separate from the body of the stem. In severe cases a limb will become completely girdled and everything above that point will die; in cases of moderate damage the bark splits and rolls back but not to the point of girdling the branch. Such injury is deceptive in that affected branches may not die until the following summer, going unnoticed in the meantime while hidden by foliage.

Sometimes freezing conditions will only split the bark without causing it to separate from the core. These wounds often callous over and allow the plant to function normally, but until the cracks heal they provide easy entry to fungus infections. Grafting wax or even paraffin painted onto these cracks will aid in their healing process and prevent diseases from entering.

*SUCKERS from understocks of grafted plants can eventually overpower top growth if not removed.*

Although some rhododendrons damaged by winter cold may sprout from their bases if you cut them down, there is usually no effective remedy for injury caused by freezing. Your best line of defense is to balance the growth of your rhododendrons and azaleas with the growing season in your area (see pages 25-28) and to provide winter protection, where necessary, for your plants (page 29).

## FAILURE TO BLOOM

The plant with no flowers—or, at most, with only a suggestion of what beauty it could produce—is a shattering disappointment to the conscientious gardener and a breach of faith to the more casual grower. Fortunately, you can easily diagnose the causes of poor bloom production and apply corrective measures.

Often young rhododendron plants spend their first several years in the garden establishing a framework at the expense of flower buds. This tendency will vary somewhat according to variety; some species raised from seed may require from 5 to 15 or more years to reach blooming age. Azalea seedlings begin blooming after 3-4 years.

Shade is probably the most frequent cause of low bloom production on established plants. Sunlight or at least *light* is required to set flower buds for the following spring; too much sun burns foliage, too little cuts down on flowers. This is largely an area of trial and error, the solution depending upon your location and the varieties you are planting. For more information on sun-shade ratios, see "Site Selection" on pages 17-19).

Over-fertilization with high-nitrogen fertilizers will produce vegetative growth in place of flower buds. Unless you live in a mild-winter climate, these plants will also be more subject to winter damage. The remedy is to re-evaluate your fertilizer program: Cut down on nitrogen or eliminate it temporarily, but maintain applications of phosphorus and potassium which will promote flower formation and ripening of growth.

Rhododendrons are prodigious seed-setters, and formation of quantities of seed takes much energy that the plant would otherwise utilize in forming flower buds for the next year. An annual spring garden job, then, is to remove faded rhododendron bloom trusses (called "deadheading"), especially on young plants. Failure to do so may lead to heavy flowering every other year with few blooms in between.

# Diseases and Insect Pests

The charts on these pages describe insect and disease problems which have been known to bother rhododendrons and azaleas. A few can become major troubles, given a combination of conditions favorable to their growth; the majority of these ills, however, are infrequent garden visitors. Remember that first line defense against any plant health problem is a strong, vigorous plant.

| CHEWING INSECTS | | | | | |
|---|---|---|---|---|---|
| PROBLEM | SYMPTOM | WHAT TO USE | HOW TO USE | WHEN TO BEGIN | WHERE FOUND |
| Root Weevils (Brachyrhinus) | Scalloped leaf edges; plant wilts more than others during warm weather. Grubs girdle trunk, eat roots. | Adult Weevils: Poisoned apple bait. Grubs: Diazinon | Scatter on foliage and soil. Work into soil before planting | Summer. | Everywhere: worse in mild climates. |
| Woods Weevil | Same symptoms as *brachyrhinus* weevil damage, but these are faster, heavier feeders, active all year. | Adults: Poisoned apple bait, malathion, diazinon. Grubs: Diazinon | Scatter bait on soil weekly. Drench soil with liquids, Work into soil before planting | Throughout the year. Monthly. | Mild areas of western United States; Pacific. |
| Asiatic Beetles | Irregular holes in younger leaves, or entire leaf eaten except for midrib and veins. Grubs attack roots and trunk. | Adults: Malathion. Grubs: Diazinon | Spray foliage. Work into soil before planting | Summer. | East of Rocky Mountains. |
| Rhododendron and Azalea Leaf Miner | Small caterpillars mine tunnels and blotches in leaves, then fold back edges of tips to pupate. | Malathion, diazinon. Hand-pick if infestation is light. | Spray foliage. | As soon as you notice activity. | Pacific coast. |
| Rhododendron and Azalea Stem Borer | Tips of new growth dead or dying in summer or early fall. Next year, grub bores down stem to crown, girdle it. | Cut out and destroy dead or dying tips. | | Summer and early fall, when noticed. | Eastern United States. |
| Midge | Spotted leaves with rolled margins, malformed growth; tips of new leaves spotted red or brown. | Hand-pick and destroy infected new growth. | | As soon as you notice activity. | Eastern United States. |
| Rhododendron Borer, Clear Wing | Holes in bark near ground level, traces of "sawdust"; yellowed foliage, stunted spring growth. | Cut and burn infested branches. Insert nicotine paste in borer holes. | | When you see borer activity or damage: fall, winter. | Eastern United States. |
| Cranberry Root Worm | Crescent-shaped or sharply angled holes in leaves. | Malathion. | Spray foliage. | Bi-weekly, in summer. | Eastern United States. |
| Pitted Ambrosia Beetle | Level galleries of blackened holes near ground level; plant becomes chlorotic, wilts and dies. | Destroy heavily-infested plants. | | | Eastern United States, Pacific Northwest. |
| Centipede; Nematodes | Yellowed, weak or stunted plants; no visible signs of insect or disease damage. | Diazinon. A nematocide. | As granules before planting. As a solution after planting. | | Everywhere. |

## SUCKING INSECTS

| PROBLEM | SYMPTOM | WHAT TO USE | HOW TO USE | WHEN TO BEGIN | WHERE FOUND |
|---|---|---|---|---|---|
| Rhododendron Lace Bug, Azalea Lace Bug (Lacewing Fly) | Grayish, mottled leaf surface; dark brown varnish-like spots on undersurface where nymphs hatch; prevalent in sun but not in shade. | Cygon. Malathion, diazinon. Move plant to shadier location. | Every 4-6 weeks. Spray foliage twice, at 10-day intervals. | When nymphs emerge. | Eastern United States, Pacific Northwest. |
| Rhododendron White Fly, Azalea White Fly | Yellow mottled leaf surface, flies and larvae on undersurface. | Cygon. Malathion, diazinon. | Every 4-6 weeks. Spray foliage twice, at 10-day intervals. | Early spring, early fall. | Eastern United States, Pacific Northwest. |
| Spider Mites (Red Spider) | White stippling on leaf surface, dried or burned appearance as damage increases; webbing on leaf undersurface. | Cygon. Malathion, diazinon. | Every 4-6 weeks. Spray foliage twice, at 10-day intervals. | When you notice infestation. | Everywhere. |
| Scale | Cottony white scale on stems and undersides of leaves. | Nymphs: cygon; malathion; diazinon. Adults: summer oil spray; combine the two for control of both. | Spray foliage and stems thoroughly. | Spring. Summer. | Everywhere. |
| Aphids | Insects are visible on new growth. | Malathion, diazinon. Systemics. | Spray foliage every 4-6 weeks. | Whenever aphids appear. | Everywhere. |
| Thrips | Gray-white mottling on leaf surface, minute dark dots underneath; flower thrips shorten the life of blooms. | Malathion. Systemics. | Spray foliage, flower buds 2 or 3 times at 10-day intervals every 4-6 weeks. | Whenever thrips appear; before buds open, for flower thrips. | Everywhere. |
| Cyclamen Mite | Minute mites enter new leaf and flower buds, produce distorted, stunted leaves, discolored flowers; greenhouse azaleas especially susceptible. | Diazinon, summer oil sprays. | Spray new growth 2 or 3 times at 10-day intervals. | Whenever mites appear. | Everywhere. |
| Mealy Bug | Usually a greenhouse pest; white, mealy-looking insects in leaf axils and in buds. | Malathion. | Spray plant 2 or 3 times at 10-day intervals. | Whenever mealy bugs appear. | Everywhere. |

## DISEASES

| PROBLEM | SYMPTOM | WHAT TO USE | HOW TO USE | WHEN TO BEGIN | WHERE FOUND |
|---|---|---|---|---|---|
| Leaf Spot (Cercospora) (Septoria) | Leaves have: purplish black spots. yellow spots, brown centers. | Fermate, *benlate. Zineb, maneb, *benlate. | Spray foliage. | When fungus appears. | Everywhere. |
| Rust | Orange-red dots on underside of leaves. | Fermate, phygon, actidione (burns some varieties). | Spray foliage. | | Everywhere (different species). |

Diseases...

| PROBLEM | SYMPTOM | WHAT TO USE | HOW TO USE | WHEN TO BEGIN | WHERE FOUND |
|---------|---------|-------------|------------|---------------|-------------|
| **Leaf Gall (Exobasidium)** | Malformed thick, fleshy new growth. | Hand-pick galled foliage. Captan, zineb, ferbam, maneb. | Spray foliage, 2-3 times at 3-week intervals. | When new growth first appears. | Everywhere. |
| **Phytophthora Blight** | Water-soaked lesions on leaves become brown or silver-spotted; brown cankers form on new growth which then wilts. | Cut out infected stems, remove shade and high humidity. Zineb, fermate, parzate. | Spray foliage. | Right after bloom and 2 weeks later (preventive); 2 times at 2-week intervals (for infection). | Anywhere that humidity is high. |
| **Powdery Mildew** | White or gray, powdery or mealy coating on leaves, tender stems; plants are most susceptible under conditions of high humidity, crowding, poor air circulation, shade; most common on deciduous azaleas. | *Benlate, actidione, dinocap. | Spray foliage and stems. | When fungus appears. | Everywhere. |
| **Phomopsis Leaf Spot and Canker** | Brown spots with silver center and red-brown edges, less than an inch across. | Cut and burn diseased branches and leaves. | | When fungus appears. | Everywhere. |
| **Rhododendron and Azalea Petal Blight** | Brown or watery-spotted petals which rapidly progress to slimy brown flowers. | PCNB, Ferbam. Zineb, acti-dione RZ, nabam compounds, (Dithane D-14, parzate liquid) | Drench soil. Spray flowers, 2 or 3 times a week. | Fall, before rains. When flowers begin to open. | Southeastern United States to California. |
| **Botrytis Petal Blight** | Gray-brown mold on petals, common on weakened or aging flowers; flowers not slimy. | Decrease shade, improve air circulation. Thylate (leaves residue). | Spray on flowers. | When infection appears. | Humid climates; East, South, Northwest. |
| **Bud Blast** | Buds turn brown during winter, hang on for 2-3 years; usually on wild rhododendrons only. | Pick and destroy infected buds. Captan. | Spray buds. | Summer and fall. | East, Pacific Northwest. |
| **Wilt (Phytophthora, Pythium)** | Plant wilted in early morning of a cloudy day, leaves are dull olive green; brown discoloration of wood beneath bark; no white feeder roots. | Koban, terrazole. Improve drainage and aeration before replanting in same location. | Drench soil. | When you spot symptoms. | Anywhere, in over-moist soil. |
| **Damping-off and Basal Canker (Rhizoctonia, Pythium)** | Same as *Phytophthora* Wilt but without brown discoloration beneath bark; attacks stems and fine roots. | Decrease water, improve drainage and air circulation. *Benlate, thiram. | Drench soil | When you spot symptoms. | Anywhere, in over-moist soil. |
| **Armillaria Root Rot (Oak Root Fungus)** | Yellow drooping leaves, white fan-shaped fungus under bark at or below soil level; black strands closely pressed to larger roots, below soil level of main stem. | Expose root crown to air: (this may prolong plant's life). Remove all old roots in soil before replanting in area where plant has died; improve drainage and aeration at same time. | | | Anywhere, in over-moist soil. |

*Benlate: This is a new systemic fungicide which may be of limited availability for a while. Experimental results indicate it to be extraordinarily effective—even curing infected plants as well as being a good preventive measure. "Dexon" (sometimes hard to find in small quantities) will control the few diseases (*fusarium and phythium*) that Benlate doesn't touch. The two in combination promise to provide a nearly complete control for soil-borne diseases of rhododendrons and azaleas.

# Landscaping with Rhododendrons and Azaleas

### Distinctive flowers, foliage provide all-year attraction

When the landscape architect thinks of rhododendrons or azaleas, he sees them in all their varied sizes and forms as well as their flower colors. And few groups of plants can offer the extreme variety of flower, foliage, and growth forms that you will find here: ground covers with needle-like leaves to forest patriarchs 60-80 feet high in their native lands, and the complete range of colors save for absolutely true blue.

*YELLOW RHODODENDRONS brighten an entryway in spring, give it elegance with foliage during year.*

## Rhododendrons In Variety

New rhododendron enthusiasts—more familiar, perhaps, with evergreen or deciduous azaleas—often regard the rhododendron as a compact, heavy-foliaged shrub, bearing fat buds, ready to produce spectacular giant trusses of flowers. To them, the difference between one rhododendron and another is scarcely more than the differences between hybrid tea rose varieties.

The big thrill in rhododendrons comes when you realize that in addition to the "hybrid tea rose" types there are also "floribunda" sorts and wildlings in infinite variety. There are rhododendrons you can use as you would azaleas or floribunda roses in low hedges dividing garden areas and in borders. There are dwarf types for the east or north-facing rock garden. A few rhododendrons are effective when trained to grow on a trellis or flat against a protected wall. The larger sorts are effective as screens or background shrubs in a wide border, while the handsome leaves of many of these kinds make them logical choices for an entrance planting. Many are so attractive in form and foliage that they would be cherished even if they were never to bloom.

## Bountiful Azaleas

Azaleas with their cheerful variety of colors are familiar to many people—if only from florist plants given on special occasions. However, gardeners whose chief exposure has been to Belgian Indica florist sorts have an azalea surprise waiting.

Although azaleas can't offer quite the range of plant, foliage, and flower types that rhododendrons do (remember that azaleas constitute but 1 out of 43 *series* in the group of plants called *rhododendrons:* see page 10), they can easily fit into

*SPRINGTIME DRAMA with Snow Azalea (R. mucronatum) in foreground, hybrid rhododendrons planted along the house. Select sorts that bloom from early to late and you can maintain flowers for months.*

as many landscape situations. There are deciduous kinds which provide a second season of interest with fall foliage color; you have a number of sorts which can serve as no-traffic ground covers, azaleas which are compact or ones that are willowy, plants wider than tall or the reverse, and some which will reach 12-15 feet high when well-grown.

Unobtrusive and neat out-of-bloom, azaleas can become sheets of color from winter (in mild climates) through spring. Appearing "at home" in plantings near water, they are also prime subjects for Oriental gardens since their structure can be guided easily into characteristic horizontal planes. Singly or in groups, azaleas in containers will dramatically enhance a patio or porch.

## Foliage Interest

Many gardeners, when shopping for a rhododendron or an azalea, are so dazzled by the profusion of flowers that they often fail to notice the variety of foliage colors and finishes which can be as effective in the landscape (although more subtly) as the floral display. Just a little browsing will disclose a wide range of greens—light to very dark,

*ELEGANT SETTING is created by soft, luxuriant conifers for a brilliant orange deciduous azalea.*

glossy to soft non-glossy finishes—and some leaves which are actually more blue or gray than they are green. With appropriate background and companion plantings, these shrubs can be like jewels in an expensive setting, in *and* out of bloom. Foliage of many deciduous azaleas—often bronze-tinted as the new leaves unfold—puts on a spectacular display in October, turning to red, gold, orange, or deepest burgundy.

A number of rhododendrons have additional foliage interest which can be exploited by the clever gardener. The undersides of the leaves in some species and varieties are covered with a peach-fuzz hair called *indumentum,* often in shades of orange, bronze, or silver to contrast with the upper green surface. Planted where you can look up at the plant (and, hence, under the leaves) the effect can be striking. And then, there are those rhododendrons whose new growths in orange, red, bronze, or chocolate rival the floral display they follow.

## Extending The Season

Most nurseries which carry "a few" rhododendrons offer the time-honored Dutch and English

*AZALEAS, FERNS, AND GNARLED TRUNKS of an old azara tree combine to create a breathtaking display.*

*ROCK GARDENS, especially on sloping ground, can be showplaces for alpine and dwarf rhododendrons.*

*FIERY BLOOMS of deciduous azaleas add zest to a woodsy path. Fall foliage color can repeat display.*

*CONGENIAL COMPANIONS in appearance, cultural demands, season of bloom are camellias and azaleas.*

hybrids, all of which come into glorious bloom at about the same time. The offerings of azaleas are frequently little better. What many gardeners fail to realize, therefore, is that there are rhododendrons and azaleas which will extend the blooming period on both sides of midseason: from January to September in mild climates, March through July where winters are severe. Check the lists on pages 68-78 for season of bloom.

With careful plant selection you can maintain a particular garden vista in flower for several months, simply by interplanting individuals that have different bloom seasons. You could vary the mood of such a planting, if you wish: the earliest display might feature yellow, orange, cream, and salmon colors; this could be followed by reds, pinks, and blush whites, finishing with lavenders, purples, violets, and cream. Remember to shelter buds and flowers of early-blooming sorts from morning sun if winter mornings are freezing; conversely, where summers are hot, the late-blooming kinds will require midday shade.

## Landscape Potential

Considering the variation in growth types, the landscape uses are limitless. Generally, azaleas appear more lightweight than the average rhododendron *hybrid* but both can be equally effective for many of the same landscape purposes: Hedges, massed shubs, woodland plantings, jewel-like specimens, and striking Oriental effects—all of these and more are not only possible with rhododendrons and azaleas, they will be admirably realized.

One word of caution: consider the ultimate size of the plant you select, and how long it will take to attain it. Too many windows have been swallowed up by ill-chosen foundation plantings, too many potentially-shapely specimen plants have developed into grotesque parodies through competition for space. Although rhododendrons and azaleas are easy to move, this should not deter you from choosing and planting wisely. You'll save yourself labor in the years that follow.

*SINGLE RHODODENDRON can be a standout when its color and texture contrast with associated plants.*

*RHODODENDRON 'BOW BELLS' shows off in foreground planting with dwarf pine, natural boulders.*

*SNOW AZALEA (R. mucronatum) creates a pleasant transition from house to lawn under low windows on east or north side. Many evergreen azaleas and smaller rhododendrons can be massed in this fashion.*

RHODODENDRONS, AZALEAS, AND WATER create images of the Orient or Deep South plantation gardens.

TALL, OPEN TREES often provide the right amount of sunlight as light patterns change during the day.

WELL-GROWN RHODODENDRONS form an effective backdrop for border of mixed spring flowers.

# Container Plants: Portable Color

## Dramatic emphasis when and where you want it

Should you let your rhododendrons and azaleas go to pot? Before you say "No," consider the advantages to be gained from even one or two choice specimens growing vigorously in containers.

**Cultural Advantage.** In some marginal areas of rhododendron and azalea culture a container-grown plant may be a practical solution to the influences which create the "margin". Hot, dry summers, alkaline soil or water, and poorly-drained soil are three negative factors which often

*EVERGREEN AZALEA 'ALBION' needs only green lawn and shrubs to set off its white flowers.*

may be circumvented by your providing a container micro-environment.

**Landscape Flexibility.** If you are growing rhododendrons or azaleas for the benefit of their flowers alone, what could be a happier event than suddenly decorating your patio with a tubbed specimen in full bloom? You can even maintain your own flower show for several months if you grow a number of varieties whose blooming periods overlap: Waning performers can be carried off stage to the lathhouse or other shady garden area, to be replaced by another variety just coming on strong. For good foliage, a healthy rhododendron or azalea can compete with the best of container plants, so that you can think of them as prime decorative items during the months out-of-bloom as well (see page 41). Should you discover that, even with proper soil, planting, and water, your container plant is receiving too much (or not enough) sun, too much wind or winter cold, or just doesn't look as good as you had thought it would in that location—you can move it, without any of the effort of digging and replanting.

**Variety of Forms.** Although mention of rhododendrons or azaleas may bring to mind the image of "basic shrub," some attention to variety selection or minor pruning can often provide you with plants of great structural beauty. Rhododendron species in the Edgeworthii, Maddenii, and Cinnabarinum series and hybrids of these frequently make leggy, even vine-like, plants which can be especially attractive espaliered informally against a wall. Most azaleas need only slight encouragement to develop an Oriental appearance much like a large bonsai. You can also find small-growing rhododendron species and hybrids which will cascade over the edge of a pot or tub, azaleas which you can use in hanging baskets for eye-level color, and handsome azaleas or small rhododendrons grown as standards for formal or dramatic effects.

FORMAL TREATMENT but informal effect: white evergreen azalea against backdrop of red bricks.

SIMPLE WOOD CONTAINER doesn't compete for attention with rhododendron. This is 'Madame Mason.'

## CONTAINER CULTURE

All that has been stressed in Chapters 2 and 3
about root environment and soil correction ap-
plies here with even greater force. In a container,
roots are restricted to making the best of whatever materials you have provided for them; there
is never the modifying influence, found in the
garden, of surrounding soil which can affect overall texture, acidity, and moisture content in the
immediate root area. The type of growing medium
you give your container plant will determine its
ability to assimilate water and fertilizers, and to
successfully endure occasional inattention.

### Soil Preparation

Predictably, the accent is on porosity but good
water retention. Several combinations of ingredients in various proportions will satisfy the needs
of your rhododendron or azalea, but once again
peat moss is a featured component. Remember,
though, the cautions that go with use of peat moss
(see page 20): Before using peat, moisten it
thoroughly (knead water into the peat with your
hands, then squeeze out excess); thereafter, never
let peat moss dry out completely. If you do let it
go dry and your plant lives through it, you face

the problem of remoistening peat. Since you cannot knead water into peat once a plant is growing
in it, you will have to submerge the container in
water containing a wetting agent until the peat
absorbs moisture again. An hour or two should be
sufficient with a wetting agent added. Some rhododendrons will die in as little as 6 hours if their
roots are completely submerged.

A planting mix of at least 50% organic matter
is essential; 75% organic is generally more satisfactory and is more often used. Some growers
plant in straight peat moss, but plants grown in it
require closer attention to watering and fertilizing.

Peat moss, ground bark, leaf mold, sand, and
sandy loam are favorite components of rhododendron and azalea container mixes. A combination
of 50% peat moss, 25% leaf mold, and 25% sand
provides adequate moisture retention, acid reaction, and sharp drainage, respectively. You could
reduce peat and sand proportions somewhat and
add ground bark to this mixture; bark retains some
moisture (as does peat) but drains sharply (like
sand). If you are sure your garden soil is sandy
loam you can use it, but never to exceed 20% of
your total mix; the remaining 80% should then
consist entirely of organic materials.

## AZALEAS AS BONSAI

Because many evergreen azaleas tend to carry their foliage in horizontal tiers, careful pruning can accentuate the planar appearance—creating an Oriental feeling with plants in the garden or actual bonsai plants in suitable containers. These photographs illustrate what selective pruning and shaping did to a well-grown nursery specimen of the Kurume azalea 'Hexe'.

The upper right photograph shows the azalea just as it came from the nursery: 1½ feet above soil level, 2 feet wide. Even though the plant is bushy you can see several planes of growth.

At the lower left you have the same plant after a first shaping was done to remove weaker, twiggy growth and expose the basic framework. The vigorous new growth on the top right-hand side of the plant was removed in this step to keep the azalea in balance and of a good size for a bonsai specimen. If you were shaping this plant for a spot in your garden you might leave some of the new growth to increase the plant's overall size; this would be shaped later, when it begins to bush out.

If you cannot give bonsai subjects the constant attention they require you will have much better results growing these specimens in larger containers (see Chapter 6) or out in the garden.

EVERGREEN AZALEA 'HEXE' as found in the nursery.

FIRST SHAPING is made to expose plant's framework.

FINAL FORM accentuates horizontal growth habit.

Gardeners in the East and South need to pay special attention to the texture and aeration of a container mixture (see cautions under "In Summer Rainfall Areas...", below ). This precludes the use of any garden soil or fine-textured materials (some peats, sand) which would become too saturated or pack down.

## In Summer Rainfall Areas . . .

Especially where summer rainfall coincides with hot, humid weather gardeners should consider rhododendrons or azaleas in containers a strictly experimental project. Special attention must be paid to the *aeration* of a container soil mixture. Without this consideration, plants in containers may decline from suffocated roots or from attacks of the Rhododendron Wilt fungus which thrives in a warm, damp condition. For these reasons you should employ coarse-textured materials in your container soil to provide ample air space between particles. Bark chips and perlite are two materials which will do this, although each is nutritionally inert and would need to be augmented with coarse leaf mold or surface litter from acid woodlands. Planting your rhododendrons or azaleas in tubs or other *large* containers will greatly improve the unfavorable heat/moisture conditions often found in smaller containers.

## Watering

Your greatest responsibility to a container-grown rhododendron or azalea is attention to proper watering. You should never let it dry out nor should the soil remain saturated. (If you have prepared a planting mixture according to the preceding directions, soggy soil should never be a problem.) Watering schedules will vary according to daily weather fluctuations and the planting mix used.

With all container-grown plants you are likely to encounter a gradual buildup of harmful salts in the planting mix. These salt accumulations may appear as a white deposit on the soil surface, or as plant damage: Chlorosis, leaf burn, or defoliation are common symptoms. To offset this damage, avoid shallow watering (give plants enough water so that some excess runs out the bottom of the container), and periodically flush out the planting mix. Every month, if your water supply is alkaline or has a high mineral salt content, fill the container with water several times until it runs freely out the drainage hole. Once every three months is sufficient where water quality is good.

## Fertilizing

With up to three-fourths of its rooting medium composed of nutritionally inert materials, your container-grown rhododendron or azalea depends on you for regularly scheduled fertilizer applications. There are a number of products, both granular and liquid, which are especially formulated for acid-loving plants generally or for rhododendrons and azaleas in particular. Any one of these will be satisfactory for your container plants, as nitrogen is present in the required ammonium form (see page 26) and the fertilizers are designed to maintain an acid soil condition when used according to directions.

If you garden where freezing winters are the rule and you intend to leave your container-grown azalea or rhododendron outdoors during winter, you will want to observe the timing of fertilizer applications, discussed on pages 25-26, to avoid late season growth that would be susceptible to cold damage. In mild climates, you can extend monthly applications into autumn. The basic fertilization schedule would begin just before bloom and continue once a month for at least three months thereafter. Liquid fertilizers, in recommended dilutions, are the safest to use on container plants: you avoid the risk of burning plants which is possible by applying too much dry fertilizer.

NOVEL TREATMENT allows evergreen azaleas to be enjoyed at eye level. Keep plants out of windy spots.

# Guiding Your Plants' Development

Pruning and training give you well-shaped plants

Mention pruning, and it brings to mind the picture of a gardener-turned-crusading-surgeon, performing complex operations to correct misguided growths of the past years. Actually, if you have watched over your rhododendrons and azaleas since their infancy—guiding their progress by judicious pinching—your pruning chores will be limited to emergency cases. Of course, if you have inherited a garden with rangy old specimen plants or having shrubs that were planted with no respect for their ultimate sizes, you will need to know how to bring these rough gems back to their deserved polish as garden ornaments.

*OLD 'PINK PEARL' RHODODENDRONS were eighteen feet tall. Cut back to two feet they sprouted quickly.*

## Pinching: Preventive Maintenance

Some rhododendrons are naturally leggy, while others branch readily and grow into a bushy form. However, when you understand how rhododendrons grow you need not let nature take its course. By pinching or breaking out leaf buds in the first two or three years of growth, you can shape potentially leggy plants into well-balanced specimens.

A typical leggy plant looks like the drawing on the next page after four cycles of growth. Occasional branching will occur but in many cases stems will continue to form with no branches.

The terminal buds (at points A) are leaf buds; in the spring these will begin to extend upward in a slim sharp point. If undisturbed they will break into leaf and grow a stem that is from several inches to a foot long depending on the species or hybrid and culture. As this growth cycle is completed in May or June, the leaves attain full size and growth stops while the wood hardens. This new shoot forms terminal buds (B) which may be either leaf or flower buds.

If buds at B are leaf buds and are left alone, the plant will produce another cycle of growth (3) without branching. If the plant is growing vigorously, two cycles (or more, in mild climates) of growth (2 and 3) may occur in one year—one cycle completed in May or June and the next in July or August. The fourth growth cycle, in the following spring, may continue without branching as in 4, or produce branches as in 4a.

In order to encourage branches to form, pinch terminal bud unless it is a round, fat, blunt-tipped flower bud. Do this as growth begins to elongate in spring. This will force several shoots to develop from dormant eyes in the lower leaf axils. A plant hormone is produced by leaf buds which inhibits development of dormant buds along the stem; flower buds do not produce this hormone, which is why a number of shoots usually grow from the lower leaf axils on branches which have flowered. If you are training a young plant (12"-18" at time of purchase), continue this pinching procedure after each growth cycle for two or three years. By then you will have a well filled-out shrub that will produce many more flower buds than one of a similar age left to its own devices.

After this initial training your rhododendron's basic structure is established. Occasionally you will need to pinch leaf buds which would grow to unbalance the plant; however, since healthy rhododendrons produce more terminal flower buds and less terminal leaf buds as the plants grow older, your training duties will steadily decrease.

## Pruning: Restorative Maintenance

The gardener who has inherited a planting of rhododendrons or azaleas frequently faces problems which require solutions more drastic than the procedures outlined above. For want of early training these shrubs may have reached a gangly middle-age, marring the landscape or hiding windows that they were never meant to cover. Or, perhaps the previous gardener, full of good intentions, had overwatered, overfertilized, or planted his rhododendrons and azaleas in more shade than they required; singly or in combination these conditions can produce rangy, unbranched plants. To restore these plants to their rightful attractiveness you will need pruning shears and courage.

## Pruning Methods

Growth buds on rhododendron plants form in the leaf *axils* (where leaf joins stem). Leaves are produced in clusters or rosettes at the ends of branches and usually persist for several years. Consequently, a three-year-old unbranched stem may have three or more rosettes of leaves: one at the branch terminal and the others lower on the branch, with bare stem between each one. Small scars along bare sections of stem are not dormant growth eyes but are from bud scales which enclosed the leaf bud before it elongated.

If you need to perform only minor repairs in order to shape up your rhododendron, make your cuts just above the leaf rosettes and new growth will emerge from the dormant eyes there.

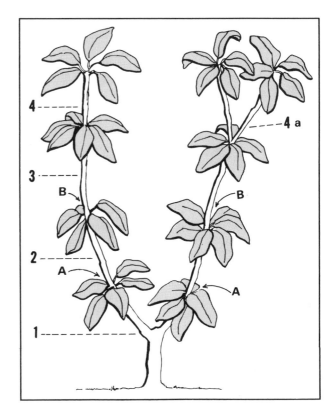

FOUR CYCLES OF GROWTH in young rhododendron. Leggy appearance could be improved with training.

Major surgery, on the other hand, requires more time and observation. When you have to cut into a branch below any leaf rosettes, look for faint rings on the bark which mark the ends of previous growth periods where there once were leaves. Careful inspection should reveal small bumps which are growth buds under the bark. Make your cuts just above the rings so that dormant buds below them will be stimulated into growth.

If you can't find any rings or dormant buds on bare branches, make your cuts wherever you must in order to shape your rhododendron; later, when new growth starts, remove all stubs down to the new growth. As a general rule, however, don't leave branch stubs above leaves or dormant eyes; they only die back to the point where new growth emerges.

Should you plan to renew a rhododendron by heavy pruning, you will get best results by removing one-third of the plant each year over a three year period. The entire plant may be cut back in one operation—and sometime you may have to treat a damaged plant this way—but you lose all flowers for a year or two and run a greater risk of losing the plant. Be sure to cut out old weak stems entirely. These will not improve under better care

## PRUNING AZALEAS

Unlike rhododendrons, azaleas have growth buds all along their stems, just under the bark surface. As a result, new growth will originate close to any cut you make.

Most evergreen azaleas require little pruning other than removal of weak or dead wood and whatever trimming is necessary to keep them shapely and within bounds. If a compact rather than open and irregular plant is desired, you can cut back some of the heavier limbs to a foot or less; from these stumps will arise strong new shoots to fill in the plant. Certain deciduous azaleas (Ghent, Knap Hill, and Mollis Hybrids) remain youthful and productive if you systematically remove old declining wood each year. At any indication of reduced vigor, cut the weakening stem to the ground; new growth will soon replace it.

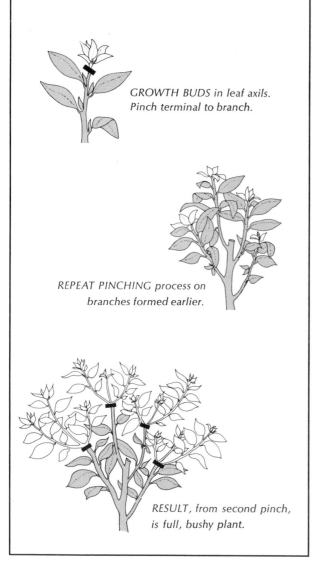

GROWTH BUDS in leaf axils. Pinch terminal to branch.

REPEAT PINCHING process on branches formed earlier.

RESULT, from second pinch, is full, bushy plant.

and are best replaced by new growth which will respond to good culture.

Dormant buds should begin to grow within a month on smaller limbs or ten weeks on tall main trunks. Occasionally, an old plant given this treatment will fail to put out any new growth; in these cases, reduce unpruned branches to the height of those pruned. Some growers have found that an application at this time of a fertilizer containing only nitrogen and phosphorus (such as 16-20-0) will stimulate new growth on a heavily-pruned rhododendron that is reluctant to break from old, bare wood. If the plant still refuses to grow, this usually indicates it was severely weakened by insects, disease, or malnutrition. When this happens, you can generally assume that you're better to start anew with a young vigorous plant, giving it careful training during its formative years.

Certain species and named rhododendron hybrids respond poorly or not at all to pruning. Members of the Falconeri series (and "tree" rhododendrons in general) will not produce new growth from bare wood; rhododendrons in the Thompsonii series also resent pruning. Smooth-barked rhododendrons make little, if any, growth from stumps, while the following hybrids will not give you multiple shoots from below a pruning cut: Alice, Bagshot Ruby, C. B. van Nes, Mrs. C. B. van Nes, and Prometheus. All of these species and hybrids must be trained from youth in order to become well-balanced, compact plants.

### When To Prune

Winter or early spring is the preferred pruning season in mild climates; in spring, after frost no longer threatens, is best where winters are severe. Because dormant growth buds start to mature following pruning, the winter or early spring operation will have them ready to grow when the growing season begins. This is especially important in areas having inhospitable winters, as it gives new growth the longest possible growing and maturing season before the onset of fall cold weather. Avoid fall pruning in cold-winter climates: Cold damage is more severe around pruning wounds than on unpruned parts of the plants.

Cutting rhododendron trusses for spring bouquets is an excellent way to do some minor pruning to shape up a plant. Irregular growths of the last year or two which destroy the symmetry of a plant are especially good candidates for cut flowers. Remember to make all cuts just above a rosette of leaves.

## PRUNING FOR SPECIAL EFFECTS

Any rhododendron which grows rapidly and has flexible stems can, with little effort, be trained as a standard or an espalier. Either treatment makes a handsome container subject, but both can serve equally well as permanent landscape items. Rhododendron hybrids from species in the Edgeworthii, Maddenii, and Cinnabarinum series are especially suitable for these treatments. If you garden where winters are mild you can grow them outdoors. In colder climates they make handsome greenhouse subjects. The standard is being created from a plant of R. 'Lady Alice Fitzwilliam'; the espalier (lower right) is R. 'Fragrantissimum.'

**As a standard...**

FIND a dominant, fairly straight stem. If none, fan branches and train against a trellis or wall.

REMOVE all lower branches and stake the trunk at point where three or four branches grow fairly close.

**As an espalier...**

CUT OUT dead, weak, and crossing branches; shorten ones that are too long. Rub off all sprouts on trunk.

HANDSOME WALL DECORATION is possible with rhododendron espalier; use sorts with relaxed growth.

# Propagation

## How to increase a favorite plant

Vegetative propagation is the centuries-old art (and skill) of producing self-sustaining plants from stems, leaves, buds, or roots of another. Usually this is done to obtain more plants of a given species or hybrid, although new sorts may be developed from stems which have produced flowers or fruit that unexpectedly differ from the normal color or form. Some azaleas frequently exhibit these "sports" and many fine new individuals have been obtained by propagating them.

Although plantsmen have devised many different techniques for vegetatively reproducing favorite ornamental plants, these techniques can be separated into two general categories: 1) those which produce new plants growing on their own roots and, 2) those in which the top growth is supported by roots of a strong-growing but less-desirable individual. All cuttings and layers fall in the first category, while grafting and budding represent the second.

### CUTTINGS

Cuttings of rhododendrons and azaleas may be taken at any time after the current season's growth has become firm but is still somewhat flexible and the tip leaves are not quite fully grown. Commercial growers, concerned with high percentage of success, often observe rather precise timing in taking cuttings; this timing depends upon the grower's location, weather conditions that year, and the individual sorts to be propagated. Thus, some may be ready for propagation as early as July while others will be best in September or later.

If your soil is dry, irrigate the plants a day before you plan to take cuttings. It is important that cuttings be full of moisture and lose as little as possible from the time they are taken until roots form. Early morning is the preferred time for the operation; keep the cuttings in covered containers or plastic bags until ready to plant.

Ease of rooting is associated with a high concentration of carbohydrates in the plant tissues. Consequently, the best cuttings come from plants making moderate—not lush—growth. Take neither the largest nor the smallest stems from the sides of the plant; cuttings from the plant's north side or

**1 YEAR OLD**
**3 YEARS OLD**
**2 YEARS OLD**

*THREE SEEDLINGS of a dwarf rhododendron show change in size according to age. Oldest has flower buds.*

from a shaded exposure are best. If you wish to insure a ready supply of good cuttings, pinch out the terminal growth bud from the new growth produced after a stem flowers; several shoots may develop in a second growth flush which will be of proper size and condition in summer or early fall. Remove the cutting stems to their point of origin; additional new growth next season will come from below this point.

## Preparing The Cuttings

After you have taken the cuttings from the parent plant, shorten them to 2½-4 inches and remove any leaves that would be buried in the rooting medium. For rhododendrons, retain all leaves in the terminal rosette (as long as there are at least three) and shorten these by ⅓ to ½. Then, make two 1-inch-long slices on opposite sides of the cutting stem—just through the bark to the base of the cutting. Roots will form from these wounded areas which will give you a heavy, well-balanced root system to anchor the plant. Be sure, however, that the cuts are deep enough to expose wood; cuts that are too shallow may heal over without rooting. Finally, dip the cuttings in a liquid or powdered rooting hormone.

## Leaf-Bud Cuttings

If you have only a leaf with a portion of stem attached, you can still start a new plant of a favorite rhododendron. This is an efficient method for utilizing "scraps" from normal cutting preparation in which you slice off an inch or so of bark, frequently containing a leaf and growth bud. All you need is a leaf with axillary bud attached to ¾-1 inch of bark, or a section of stem cut above and below the leaf with bud.

Insert these leaf-bud cuttings in the same medium you use for normal cuttings and give them the same treatment thereafter. One word of caution: don't cover the growth bud when you insert a bark sliver or stem segment into the rooting bed.

Some leaf-bud cuttings will form roots but no top growth in the greenhouse; often these will grow after experiencing one winter outdoors. In transplanting these be sure not to bury the dormant buds.

## Rooting Media

Any ingredient or combination of ingredients which will provide a well-*aerated*, well-*drained*, yet *moisture-retentive* rooting medium will successfully root rhododendron and azalea cuttings under the proper atmospheric conditions. The safest medium is one which contains *only sterile ingredients*. If you also use clean containers and tools, such a mixture is not likely to become infected with damping-off fungi which, if unchecked, can destroy entire populations of new seedlings or rooting cuttings. (See page 39 for description and remedies.) Of these sterile materials, sphagnum moss is somewhat too fibrous and becomes too wet; peat moss, used alone, tends to be too soggy; sand will give the best aeration but requires frequent watering to maintain a satisfactory moisture level. Consequently, for rooting cuttings many growers prefer a mixture of clean, sharp sand and peat moss, from equal parts of each to one part peat and two of sand. Experiments have suggested that shredded styrofoam (an inert plastic foam) in equal parts with sand and peat moss helps provide superior aeration and rooting. Similarly, a combination of 50% peat moss and 50% perlite (lightweight expanded mineral kernels) has given a successful rooting environment.

The rooting media just described are devoid of nutrients, so that if you transplant rooted cuttings into any one of them you will have to supply all nutrients artificially.

A common practice is to incorporate leaf mold or garden loam into the planting mix for transplants. The proportions vary according to the texture of the loam or leaf mold, bearing in mind that aeration and moisture retention are always of prime importance. Two parts peat to one each of sand and loam is one possible mixture, or you could use equal parts peat, sand, and leaf mold.

## Rooting Environment

When you have prepared the cuttings for planting, you have a choice of methods which will induce rooting. Although there are several basic arrangements for doing this (and nearly as many modifications as there are propagators), there are two critical conditions that the various methods were designed to meet: a humid atmosphere for cuttings, and initial warmth. You cannot compromise the humidity requirement, but if you choose to propagate outdoors the warmth will gradually be sacrificed as winter approaches. Your selection of method will be governed by your available facilities and the number of cuttings you want to root.

## Indoor Propagation

You will find that cuttings root faster if you can start them in a greenhouse atmosphere in autumn. Indoors, roots will continue to grow throughout the winter months, whereas outdoors they will be delayed during winter in all but the mildest climates.

Traditionally, the propagator would place cuttings directly in the greenhouse bench and cover it with a glass sash. By supplying bottom heat from an electric heating cable, he would root the cuttings at 70-75°F, later reducing this temperature to 60°F after cuttings appeared definitely rooted. At this point he would gradually ventilate the cutting bed until new plants were fully exposed to the normal greenhouse atmosphere.

Now, experiments with polyethylene plastic sheeting have demonstrated its superiority to glass in maintaining the proper humid atmosphere. Plastic is, of course, easier to work with than glass, but more important is its ability to transmit oxygen and carbon dioxide while retaining moisture in the area it encloses. This property eliminates the need for any ventilation or frequent watering of the rooting medium.

To adapt polyethylene plastic to the traditional greenhouse method, put up a frame (wood or wire will do) which will extend 12-15 inches above the soil surface in the greenhouse bench. After you insert the cuttings and water them in, cover the frame with polyethylene so that the propagating area is completely covered by this plastic "tent." Retain moisture within the tent by tightly sealing all edges from the outside atmosphere. If this seal is maintained you should need to water the cuttings only every four to six weeks; rhododendron cuttings will root in two to three months, azaleas will be ready earlier.

## Mist Propagation

If your water supply is not alkaline (does not contain "hard" mineral salts), mist culture will give you a high percentage of successful cuttings with all but deciduous azaleas. These are better propagated in a polyethylene tent or the Nearing Frame, described next.

To set up a mist bed, install a water pipe two feet above a greenhouse cutting bench and running the length of the area you intend to use. Space mist nozzles along this pipe at intervals that will provide even mist coverage. The objective is to keep the cuttings bathed in a constantly moist atmosphere but not in a saturated condition; an electric time switch to turn the water on and off

*TWO PROPAGATING AIDS. Small greenhouse (left) is a flat with polyethylene plastic cover held up by wire hoops or hardware cloth. Nearing Frame (right) is popular in the east for rooting cuttings outdoors.*

at prescribed intervals is essential. Six seconds of mist followed by three minutes "off" is a satisfactory interval; you can adjust the timing if your cuttings become too wet or too dry. Water and air temperature should be about the same: 75-80°F. The mist system is automatically turned off during evening and started again at sunrise. A "shower curtain" of polyethylene plastic around the propagating area will reduce drafts and keep the mist contained around the cuttings.

This same mist method may also be employed outdoors in a sunny but sheltered location. There, you will have to experiment with the mist frequency to obtain the proper foggy atmosphere; it is possible you may need constant mist.

### Polyethylene Tent

For most gardeners who have no greenhouse and want to start only limited quantities of new plants at one time, a flat under a polyethylene plastic "tent" is an efficient propagating case. Ordinarily you would utilize this method outdoors where there is enough natural light for growth, but with the use of fluorescent lights you can grow cuttings indoors the year round. For indoor culture you will need two fluorescent tubes (350-400 foot-candles) in a reflector suspended over the tent, operating 18 hours a day.

First you will need to construct a framework to support the polyethylene over the flat; for this, the easiest solution is to make three arches of heavy wire and attach them to the *inside* of the flat. This will look like the framework for a covered wagon. All you have to do then is fill the flat with rooting medium, insert the cuttings and water them, and cover the framework with the plastic. Here again, be sure there are no gaps in your plastic cover through which moisture-laden air could escape. Remember that the oxygen-carbon dioxide transfer *through* the plastic is all the ventilation the cuttings need.

If you plan to leave this propagating case outside during a freezing winter, you must locate it where it will not undergo much alternate freezing and thawing. A north wall may provide some protection from temperature fluctuation; otherwise the flat should be placed in a north-facing cold frame which can be opened or closed to suit the changing weather. Since freezing and thawing (and consequent heaving of the cuttings) is hard to prevent with such a small volume of rooting medium, its greatest convenience in cold-winter climates is for propagation of sorts which would

be rooted by the time freezing weather arrives. Cuttings of deciduous azaleas in May and of conventional rhododendron hybrids in early July should be rooted by winter. You may need to water the flat before it freezes for the winter; otherwise it should need no attention until several weeks after the spring thaw.

### Outdoors: The Nearing Frame

A highly successful outdoor method of rhododendron and azalea propagation was developed and patented by Guy G. Nearing in the 1930's. Since then, the Nearing Frame patent has expired, and several other growers have made modifications to further increase the frame's efficiency. Popularity of this frame has been greatest in the eastern United States where rhododendron country invariably experiences freezing winters. There, plants grown outdoors in the Nearing Frame are often better adapted to outside conditions than are plants started in greenhouse atmospheres. For the small gardener who has time to individually care for each plant, this advantage may be of somewhat less importance than to the commercial grower with fields of young plants to protect.

**Construction.** The design is that of a cold frame with tongue-and-groove (but not watertight) floor, enclosed by two sides and a steeply sloping roof which leaves the frame open only to the north. The interior of the sides and roof are painted white to reflect the greatest possible amount of north light into the frame. The cutting bed is tightly covered by a glass sash, which maintains a humid atmosphere for the cuttings. Effectiveness of the Nearing Frame depends upon strict observance of three essentials: 1) it must face exactly due north; 2) rooting medium must be level; and 3) the glass sash should form an air-tight fit with the frame.

First, select an open northern exposure and find due north (you will need a compass); then, build a frame of whatever size you need but deep enough that the tongue-and-groove floor will be one foot below ground level. You can increase the stability of this frame by allowing the wood floor to extend 8-12 inches beyond the sides, front, and back. *Level the frame* and fill soil back in around it so that the soil slopes away from the frame.

Parts of the frame in constant contact with soil and moisture should be made from decay-resistant wood such as cypress, redwood, or treated fir; you can use almost any durable material for the sides and sloping roof so long as it will take a coat of white paint.

Next, construct the sides and roof. If your frame is 3x6 feet you can buy glass hotbed sashes to fit. The north end must be high enough to exclude all sun. For the same reason, compass finding of due north should be adjusted for any deviation at your latitude. Any sun which strikes the covering sash may overheat the air beneath and so destroy the cuttings. The sides and roof assembly may be attached to the frame or may be a separate unit securely placed around it.

**Rooting Medium.** For best results these directions for rooting mixture preparation should be followed exactly; they assure the best possible soil aeration and moisture retention. A layer of *moistened* peat moss goes into the bottom of the frame (one bushel for a 3x6-foot frame); this layer provides the constant moisture supply to the next layer in which the cuttings root. Pack it lightly and level it.

The next layer is equal parts sand and peat moss (1½ bushels of each for the 3x6-foot frame), which provides a well-drained and aerated medium for rooting. One successful east coast nurseryman has had best results (especially with hard-to-root deciduous azaleas) from a mixture of equal parts peat moss, sand, and perlite. Level this but *do not pack.* Scatter ¼-inch of sand over the sand-peat layer and saturate the contents with a diffuse stream of water until ⅛-inch briefly remains on the sand. The frame is now ready to receive the cuttings.

**Cuttings And Their Care.** Plant prepared rhododendron cuttings up to the rosette of leaves, azalea cuttings to the base of their lowest leaves. It is important that cuttings not be so long as to extend into the layer of peat beneath the rooting medium. Two-and-one-half inches is about maximum length; even cuttings as short as 1 inch may root well. Water these as before (until ¼-inch briefly remains on the sand) and close the sash. Before cold weather arrives, you will have to water the cuttings weekly, then every other week from the onset of cold weather until the ground freezes. To keep the glass sash clean for the maximum amount of light to reach your cuttings, wash off the glass each time you water. From the time the ground freezes until spring thaw, the frame requires no attention. After the thaw, resume watering at two week intervals, then every week as weather warms.

When your cuttings have grown enough roots to transplant (usually by August), gradually ventilate the cutting bed to a 1-foot opening in 10 days.

If you plan to start another crop of cuttings in your Nearing Frame, you should remove the previous rooting medium and repeat the layering process with fresh peat and sand. The aeration in the sand-peat mixture decreases during the year of propagating so that re-use will produce a lower percentage of successful rootings.

## LAYERING

For the unhurried gardener who prefers not to fuss with propagation devices, layering is the easiest means of increasing a favorite rhododendron or azalea. Until recently it was a favored method of commercial propagation in Europe but is gradually being supplanted as research uncovers ways to root cuttings of difficult kinds.

### Soil Layering

The principle is extremely simple: The stem which is to become the new plant is never completely cut from the "mother" plant, so that fluids and nutrients are continually supplied to the layered stem. The chief drawback is the time necessary for the new plant to become self-sustaining: eighteen months later is about as soon as you can expect. Azaleas root so easily from cuttings that

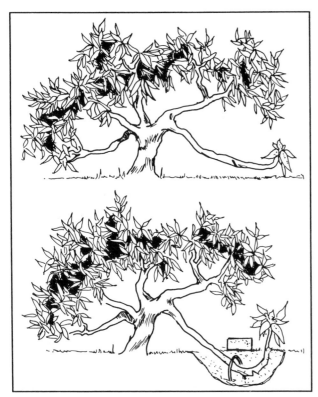

*SOIL LAYERING is easy on plants with low-hanging branches. Make cut on upper or under side.*

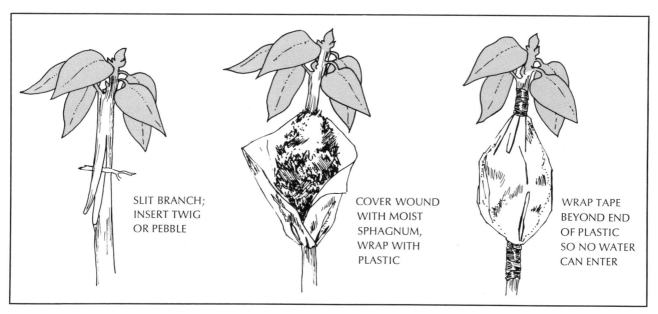

SLIT BRANCH; INSERT TWIG OR PEBBLE

COVER WOUND WITH MOIST SPHAGNUM, WRAP WITH PLASTIC

WRAP TAPE BEYOND END OF PLASTIC SO NO WATER CAN ENTER

*AIR LAYERING gives you a choice of more branches to root than does soil layering. Be sure the sphagnum is not soggy and that the polyethylene plastic is well sealed to prevent loss of moisture.*

you would probably prefer to use the glass jar method illustrated on page 60 if you want only a few plants.

First, select a flexible low branch with firm growth from the current season or previous year; dig a 3 to 4-inch deep trench in the soil below the branch. Then, make a cut half-way through the *upper* side of the branch and pin the branch in the trench with a wire "hairpin." Finally, twist the end of the branch 90 degrees, bend it upright, and rub a rooting hormone into the wound. You may want to stake the branch to hold it upright. Fill soil back into the trench (adding peat moss, sand, or leaf mold if necessary) and water it in. You can perform the layering operation at any time the ground is not frozen, although it is usually done in August when the season's growth has become firm. The damp autumn weather is favorable to rapid root formation.

### Air Layering

This method has a wider application than soil layering, if for no other reason than there are many more branches available for layering higher on the plant than there are at soil level. You use the same current-season or last year's growth for air layering, but for this method you will need sphagnum moss, polyethylene plastic, and waterproof electrical tape.

The previous year's growth may be air-layered at any time; August or later is best for current season's growth. Select the branch you want to layer, make an upward cut (toward the end of the branch) about two inches long and halfway through, and dust the cut surfaces with a rooting hormone (one for hard-to-root plants is best).

Insert a small pebble or twig in the wound to keep it open. Then, take a handful of moist sphagnum moss from which you have squeezed all excess water and press it around the stem where you made the cut. Finally, enclose the sphagnum ball in polyethylene plastic and bind the cut ends of the plastic to the stem with waterproof electrical tape until there is no collar of exposed plastic at either end. A plastic bag from which you have cut off an end is a convenient wrap; slip the tube of plastic down the stem and over the damp sphagnum, then bind with waterproof tape.

You may have rooted air layers by fall if you prepared them in spring. Freezing winters won't harm the roots in sphagnum if you leave the layers on the plant. If no root activity is evident during the first season, leave the plastic-wrapped moss on the branch; often branches will root during the second year.

Proper moisture content in the sphagnum moss is the key to success with air layering. Be sure to squeeze all extra moisture from it when you apply it to the branch, and wrap the plastic ends securely so that no extra water can enter.

Conversely, secure wrapping also insures that no moisture will escape from within the plastic, thereby drying out the rooting area.

BEST CUTTINGS from tip growth of current season—will break when bent sharply. Make a clean cut.

REMOVE LOWER LEAVES that would be buried, dip cutting in rooting hormone, and insert in rooting mix.

WATER CUTTING to settle mix; invert glass jar over it. Raise jar occasionally to admit air, prevent mold.

AZALEA'S ROOT SYSTEM shows good development after three months. Rooted in half peat moss, sand.

## GRAFTING

Rhododendron and azalea enthusiasts have for years disputed the relative advantages of own-root plants vs. grafted specimens. Recent research and experience tends to support the claims made for plants grown on their own roots, and certainly this sort of propagation is easier for the home gardener. However, there are occasions when grafted or budded plants would be superior.

The successful graft depends upon:
1) sharp tools,
2) careful matching of cambium layers in stock and scion,
3) a secure tie of scion to stock,
4) proper timing,
5) a steady hand and experience.

### Advantages to Grafting Or Budding

Difficult-to-root hybrids and species may be increased faster by grafting them onto vigorous understocks. The percentage of successful grafts will be greater than that of successful cuttings.

**Increased Soil Tolerance.** Some varieties and species are especially particular about soil texture and acidity when grown on their own roots. Grafting these individuals onto rugged, adaptable understocks (*Rhododendrons fortunei, discolor*, and 'Cunningham's White' are popular choices) allows gardeners in marginal areas to enjoy them.

**Standards** for formal effects are most easily produced by grafting or budding the desired variety onto stems of fast-growing species or hybrids.

### Green Grafting Outdoors

The newcomer to grafting will probably achieve greater success with less effort from this method. No greenhouse or similar structure is necessary, and the absolute matching of cambium layers—although desirable—is not as critical with actively growing plants.

During the growing season, whenever the spring flush of growth is half matured, you can begin your green grafting. The best understocks are two-year-old seedlings or cutting-grown plants. If you want the grafts to be as low as possible on the understock so that there will be less area from which suckers can grow, cut the understock to ½-inch of the soil level in early spring. Select the strongest sprout which grows from the stub or roots and rub out all others. By July this will be

ready for grafting. If you don't mind a higher graft, use green wood of the last growth flush without cutting down the understocks.

After you have made the grafts, covered them with damp sphagnum, and secured the plastic bags, all you need to give them is routine watering until the grafts have healed. Be careful to give the grafted plants plenty of light but no direct sun.

When it is apparent that grafts have healed, open the plastic bag but leave it in place for a few days. Following removal of the bag, leave the sphagnum on for two weeks; thereafter, treat the grafted plants as you would rooted cuttings.

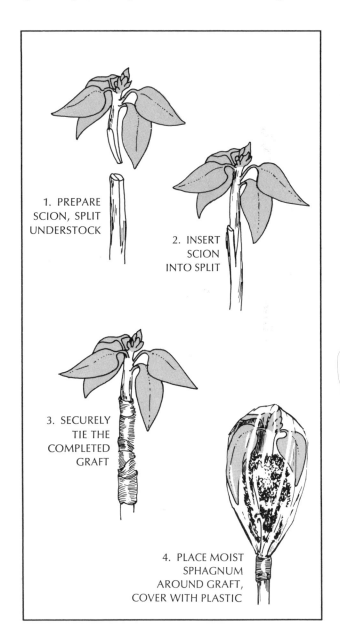

1. PREPARE SCION, SPLIT UNDERSTOCK

2. INSERT SCION INTO SPLIT

3. SECURELY TIE THE COMPLETED GRAFT

4. PLACE MOIST SPHAGNUM AROUND GRAFT, COVER WITH PLASTIC

*FOUR STEPS TO GREEN GRAFTING, the easiest method for the amateur since all is done outdoors.*

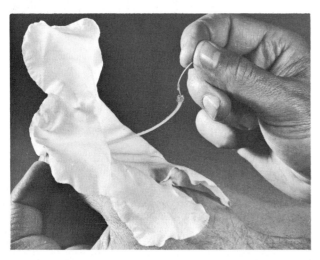

REMOVE PETALS to reduce chances of pollination by insects; this takes away their "landing field."

*TIME TO HAND POLLINATE is when pistil becomes sticky. Transfer pollen from another to stigma.*

*RIPE SEED CAPSULES at right are ready to open, yield seed. Those at left have already opened.*

## NEW PLANTS FROM SEED

You need nothing more than a covered plastic box, screened sphagnum moss, and possibly a coldframe to grow rhododendrons and azaleas from seed. The boxes act as miniature greenhouses, supplying the seedlings with the necessary warmth, moisture, and light for proper development. Almost any transparent container will do if it has a tight-fitting cover and is deep enough to hold the sphagnum and seedlings. Wash the plastic containers in a solution of 1 part chlorinated household bleach to 20 parts water to discourage fungus diseases which might get started in the enclosed atmosphere.

Moisten the sphagnum moss, squeeze it as dry as you can, and pack it firmly into the plastic boxes. Be sure to leave about 1½ inches between the container lid and the sphagnum surface for the seedling growth. Sow seeds *on* the sphagnum, then sprinkle with a *very fine mist* of water; or, press the seed gently into the seedbed to insure good contact with sphagnum. Avoid washing the seed down into sphagnum, where it won't germinate. Put the lid on the box and place it in indirect light in a room or greenhouse where temperatures remain between 70 and 80°F. Germination will begin in 1 to 4 weeks.

When it appears that no more seeds will germinate, move the boxes into more light—but not direct sun—and into a cooler area. A north window in a room where temperatures stay in the low to mid 60's is fine.

You can keep seedlings in the closed boxes for an amazing length of time, but usually you will want to transplant them into flats or pots when they have two sets of leaves. Several weeks before you transplant your seedlings, begin ventilating the boxes, with a toothpick or matchstick, prop up the lid at one end and, over a 3-week period, gradually increase the opening to about ¾ inch. Don't let the sphagnum dry out during this period; if it seems at all dry, water it. Finally, a few days with the lid off will prepare the seedlings for a move to larger containers and a different rooting medium.

A planting mixture of 40% leaf mold, 40% peat moss and 20% sand or perlite gives the transplants a well-aerated and acidic medium in which to establish their roots. Liquid fertilizer suitable for acid-loving plants may be given the seedlings every 2 to 3 weeks, from the time they have their first set of leaves.

1. *SCREEN SPHAGNUM MOSS through ¼-inch mesh, then soak in water. Squeeze it as dry as you can.*

2. *SOW SEEDS onto layer of hand-squeezed moist sphagnum; scatter them as widely as possible.*

3. *RHODODENDRON SEEDLINGS. Those in front are three weeks old; at right they have second set of leaves.*

4. *TRANSFER SEEDLINGS to flats (shown here) or individual pots as soon as they have two sets of leaves.*

# Shopping for Rhododendrons and Azaleas

## Selecting plants for lasting satisfaction

The selection of rhododendrons and azaleas for your garden should be a pleasurable, even stimulating experience. If, however, you are to avoid bewilderment at the nursery and possible future disappointment from any individuals unsuited to your garden, spend a few moments reading the lists in this chapter. From these charts you may be able to choose a number of especially suitable candidates for those choice spots in the garden—before you leave your home. Having

*RHODODENDRON SHOPPING can be exciting and colorful, but first have an idea of what sorts you want.*

narrowed your field of choice in this manner, your final decisions at the nursery will be more likely to produce plants which will give you lasting satisfaction.

### Rhododendron Quality Ratings

A number of years ago the British Rhododendron Society initiated a system of rating the quality of hybrids and species. From one to four stars indicated increasing quality; no stars denoted either a very poor sort or a hybrid which was too new or too unexceptional to be rated.

More recently—beginning in 1950—the American Rhododendron Society began a rating system of its own, similar to that used by the British but based upon evaluations made in this country. Expressed either as numbers or plus marks, these ratings are:

5—Superior
4—Above Average
3—Average
2—Below Average
1—Poor

Using the number system, a variety may be rated separately as to its flower and plant quality: 5/3 tells you the bloom is "Superior" on a plant of "Average" attractiveness.

### Hardiness Ratings

Disappointed by discrepancies between a number of British hardiness ratings and the performance in this country of hybrids so rated, the American Rhododendron Society set out to re-evaluate hybrid and species temperature tolerances. These ratings are still undergoing some modification as species and hybrids become subjected to unusual conditions. You should remember that local conditions (especially in hilly and mountainous areas) may vary considerably, the lower gardens often experiencing the lower temperatures. The *timing* of low temperatures can also determine a plant's sensitivity to cold: Cold spells which follow unusually warm weather or which strike after growth has started can damage a plant even though the temperatures fall within the rhododendron's rated hardiness.

### Season of Bloom

The months given by the American Rhododendron Society for a species' or hybrid's peak blooming date were for the rhododendron season in Portland, Oregon. There, mid-season bloom is in early May. If your mid-season is earlier or later you will have to make adjustments relative to Portland.

### Plant Size at Maturity

Dwarf—under 1½ feet
Semi-dwarf—under 3 feet
Low—under 4½ feet
Medium—under 6 feet
Tall—over 6 feet

### Evergreen Azalea Hybrids

For nearly 150 years hybridizers have worked with evergreen azaleas. The usual objective of each hybridizer was to produce a group of plants which would perform well in a particular situation: in the greenhouse, in a cold-winter climate, or in hot-summer territory. As a result, most evergreen azalea hybrids sold today can be separated into reasonably distinct groups, the members of which have similar climatic tolerances and often similar growth and flower types. Listed here are brief group descriptions with a code for each which refers to the charts on pages 74-77.

**SI—Southern Indica.** These are the garden azaleas famous throughout the Deep South. They were originally selected from the Belgian Indicas as being generally more rugged and able to perform better in full sun than most other azaleas. Somewhat hardier than Belgian Indicas, they will take temperatures from 10°-20°, although some will split bark at 20°. Most white-flowered varieties will have buds frozen at 20°. In general they grow faster, more vigorously, and taller than other kinds. You may find them sold as "Sun Azaleas."

**BI—Belgian Indica.** This is a group of hybrids originally developed for greenhouse forcing and is the usual gift azalea you will find with large, brightly-colored, double or semi-double flowers. In mild areas where lowest temperatures are between 20° and 30°, many of them serve very well as landscape plants. Their evergreen foliage is lush and full, the large flowers are profuse during the flowering season.

**K—Kurume.** These plants have been garden favorites in Japan for over a century, developed there for outdoor culture. Kurume azaleas grow rather compactly and are densely foliaged with small leaves. Although flowers are small they come out in masses, often in attractive tiers suggestive of plants in Japanese prints. They will take temperatures down to 5° or 10° and grow well outdoors in half sun, but they can not endure hot, dry wind in summer.

**GL—Glenn Dale.** These hybrids take their name from the site of the U. S. Division of Plant Exploration and Introduction Station at Glenn Dale, Maryland. They were developed to get the color and flower size of the southern azaleas on a plant that would be hardy in the mid-Atlantic states. Some grow tall and rangy, others low and compact; some have small leaves like the Kurumes; others have large leaves. Growth varies from rapid to slow. Glenn Dale hybrids grow well outdoors in half sun, and in some cases full sun. In cold winters they will drop some leaves.

**G—Gable Hybrids.** These hybrids were developed to produce evergreen azaleas of the Kurume type that would take 0° temperatures. They may lose some foliage in the low range of their tolerance, but they bloom heavily from April through May.

**Mac—Macrantha.** These azaleas include plants that are sometimes referred to as Gumpo, Chugai, and Satsuki hybrids. They are hardy to around 5° and include true dwarf, low-growing forms. Flowers are larger than those of the Kurumes; the Dai-Satsuki hybrids have blooms up to 5 inches across. All bloom late, into June.

**P—Pericat Hybrids.** This is a series of azaleas developed by Alphonse Pericat in Pennsylvania for greenhouse forcing. Possibly hybrids of Kurume and Belgian Indica varieties, they look much like the Kurumes and are about as hardy outdoors.

A typical azalea flower has five petals joined at the base to form a tube, giving the flower a trumpet or funnel shape. At the base of this trumpet or funnel there is also an outer ring of very small green sepals which are joined together. In the center of the flower are five stamens—sometimes more, but in multiples of five. This arrangement constitutes a *single* flower.

In many cases the filaments of the stamens become petal-like; then you have a *semi-double* or *double* flower, depending on the number of stamens that assume the petal-like form.

The term *hose-in-hose* means that the outer ring of normally small green sepals become large, petal-like and showy. Since they are joined into a tube at the base (like the petals) the flower appears to be inside another. In this case the stamen filaments may also become petal-like; then you have a *semi-double hose-in-hose* or *double hose-in-hose*.

*SINGLE (left), semi-double (center), and double (right) azalea flowers show how doubleness is achieved as stamens become petal-like.*

*HOSE-IN-HOSE flowers result when sepals at base of flower become petal-like; single (left), semi-double (center), and double (right) forms are possible.*

**R—Rutherfordiana.** These hybrids are the American equivalents of the Belgian Indicas, developed for greenhouse forcing. In cold areas they are still greenhouse plants, but where temperatures don't go below 20° they make attractive landscape subjects. Plants are bushy, about 2 to 4 feet high, with handsome foliage. Flowers are intermediate between the Belgian Indicas and Kurumes; they may be single, semi-double, or double.

**Br—Brooks Hybrids.** These were developed in California's Central Valley where they would have to endure hot, dry summers. They will also perform well wherever Belgian Indicas or Rutherfordianas can be grown outdoors.

**GC—Gold Cup Hybrids.** This is another California development, combining the large flowers of Belgian Indicas with the vigorous habit of the Rutherfordianas. They make good landscape plants where temperatures don't go below 20°.

### Deciduous Azalea Hybrids

Development of these hybrids began during the 1820's in Belgium and, like the evergreen azaleas, has diverged into several hybrid groups. Differences between hybrid groups here, however, are less distinct than in evergreen types, because these groups have some parent species in common.

Eight different species were used in various combinations to produce the deciduous hybrids. From America were *Rhododendrons calendulaceum, nudiflorum, viscosum, occidentale,* and *arborescens.* China contributed *Rhododendron molle,* Japan gave *R. japonicum,* and even *R. luteum* (the sometimes-notorious Pontic Azalea) was used. The Ghent Hybrids were the first group to emerge, followed by Mollis Hybrids and Occidentale Hybrids—all produced before the turn of the century. The greatest interest today centers around the Knap Hill Hybrids which had their beginnings in Anthony Waterer's Knap Hill Nursery around 1870. These hybrids feature open, squarish flowers (a contribution of *Rhododendron occidentale*) in white, cream, brilliant yellow, orange, and red, and in all shades of pink. Breeding stock from Knap Hill varieties gave rise to various strains, of which the Exbury strain of Rothschild is currently the most prominent.

A number of other hybridizers have worked with parent material from the Knap Hill Nurseries, calling the resulting seedlings by their own names (as the "Ilam Hybrids" from New Zealand) or designating the seedlings as their own "Knap Hill Hybrids." Current work with these deciduous azaleas by amateur hybridizers will probably eliminate distinctions between hybrid strains and merge all into a race of large, square-shaped flowers in the color range of Knap Hill hybrids with the addition of flowers in purple shades. All deciduous azaleas take a year or more to recover full blooming vigor after being moved.

**Kn (Knap Hill)** and **Ex (Exbury)** hybrids have the largest flowers found in deciduous azaleas (to 5 inches across, in some hybrids) and are hardy to around $-20°$.

**M—Mollis Hybrids.** These are upright plants, 4 to 5 feet tall; flowers are $2^1/2$ to 4 inches wide and are carried in clusters of 7-13.

**Gh—Ghent Hybrids.** Just about the hardiest of azaleas, many of these have taken $-25°$. Flowers are generally smaller than those of the Mollis Hybrids; upright plants reach 4-6 feet.

**Oc—Occidentale Hybrids.** These are derived from crosses of the Mollis Hybrids with the Western Azalea, *Rhododendron Occidentale*. Flowers are no larger than Mollis Hybrids, but plants grow taller—to 8 feet.

Knap Hill and Exbury strains in particular are frequently sold as unnamed or even unbloomed seedlings. For the gambler these are often very satisfactory garden ornaments, but if you want to be certain of quality and color you will want to buy named hybrids.

TWO CUTTING-GROWN PLANTS. The three-year-old is well-branched, budded; small plant is one year old.

EXBURY HYBRID AZALEA 'Oxydol,' one of the most popular whites, growing here with pines and Mahonia. All deciduous azaleas are especially attractive with a background of dark green conifers.

# Rhododendron, Azalea Hybrids

In the following charts you will find information which will help you select a rhododendron or azalea suitable for your climate and for specific landscape situations. Rhododendrons and ever-green azaleas are first separated into color groups, then the sorts in each group are listed alphabetically by name; deciduous azaleas are listed alphabetically by name in one group.

**"g" after rhododendron name signifies "group" (see page 12)**

| | | | | | RHODODENDRONS (White) |
|---|---|---|---|---|---|
| **NAME** | **HARDY TO:** | **SEASON OF BLOOM** | **HEIGHT** | **ARS RATING** | **CHARACTERISTICS** |
| Beauty of Littleworth | −5 | Early May | Tall | 4/3 | White flowers speckled with red-purple on upper petals; 4-5" across. Conical truss, dark green leaves. Vigorous, upright spreading. |
| Boule de Neige | −25 | Early May | Low | 3/4 | Pure white flowers appear in snowball-like trusses. Light green 6-inch leaves cover the rounded plant. Susceptible to Lace Wing Fly if planted in full sun. |
| Catalgla | −25 | Late May | Medium | 4/2 | White flowers in tall trusses. Dark green foliage, open plant. A selection of the white form of *R. catawbiense*. |
| Catawbiense Album | −25 | Late May | Medium | 3/3 | Rounded trusses of blush to white flowers spotted greenish-yellow. Compact, spreading plant with medium to dark green leaves. |
| Cilpinense g. | +5 | March | Semi-dwarf | 4/4 | Flowers are blush to white, funnel-shaped, in loose clusters. Shiny green leaves clothe the spreading plant. Very profuse bloom. |
| Countess of Haddington | +20 | April | Medium | 4/4 | Fragrant white flowers flushed pink are funnel-shaped, 4 inches long and 3 inches across, held in lax trusses of 3 to 4. Spreading. |
| County of York | −15 | May | Tall | 3/3 | Pale chartreuse buds open to creamy-white flowers with greenish throats; tall trusses. Deep green leaves are convex and long — up to 12 inches. Open plant habit. |
| Cunningham's White | −15 | Late May | Semi-dwarf | 2/3 | Small white flowers with greenish blotch in small, upright trusses. Many flowers. Spreading, compact plant has shiny, rather dark foliage. Tough and adaptable. Also used as an understock. |
| Dora Amateis | −15 | Late April | Semi-dwarf | 4/4 | White, green-spotted 2-inch flowers in clusters of 3-5. Rounded compact shrub with boat-shaped leaves to 3" long. Vigorous. |
| Fragrantissimum | +20 | Early April | Medium | 4/3 | Nutmeg fragrance from white funnel-shaped flowers to 4" across. Growth is willowy, flexible; can be used as a vine, ground cover, espalier, or shrub. Responds to pinching and pruning. |
| Great Lakes | −25 | Mid-May | Semi-dwarf | 3/4 | Pink buds open to 2-inch white flowers in domed trusses of 15. Medium green leaves have tan indumentum. Very compact plant. |
| Lady Alice Fitzwilliam | +20 | Mid-April | Medium | 4/4 | Fragrant white funnel-shaped flowers to 5" across. Very similar to 'Fragrantissimum' but plant is more compact and upright. |
| Loder's White | 0 | Late April | Medium | 5/5 | Pink buds open to lightly frilled white flowers. Plant is compact and spreading with 6-inch bright green leaves. Free blooming. |
| Madame Mason | −5 | Mid-May | Medium | 3/3 | Pure white with yellow blaze on upper petals. Trusses are compact, tall and conical. Dark green foliage. |
| Mother of Pearl | 0 | Mid-May | Tall | 4/3 | A sport of 'Pink Pearl' and like it in every way but color: this one opens blush pink and fades to pure white. |

Rhododendrons, white...

| NAME | HARDY TO: | SEASON OF BLOOM | HEIGHT | ARS RATING | CHARACTERISTICS |
|------|-----------|-----------------|--------|-----------|-----------------|
| Sappho | −5 | Mid-May | Tall | 3/2 | Medium-sized white flowers with conspicuous purple blotch on upper petals; compact, domed truss. Open growth habit. |
| White Pearl | +5 | Mid-May | Tall | 3/3 | Blush flowers from pink buds fade to pure white with green centers; very large domed trusses. Very vigorous plant with 7-inch dark green leaves. Sometimes sold as 'Halopeanum'. |
| Windbeam | −25 | Late April | Semi-dwarf | 4/3 | White flowers change to soft pink as they age. Lavish bloomer. Small, aromatic foliage on spreading plant. |

## RHODODENDRONS (Pink)

| NAME | HARDY TO: | SEASON OF BLOOM | HEIGHT | ARS RATING | CHARACTERISTICS |
|------|-----------|-----------------|--------|-----------|-----------------|
| Alice | −5 | Mid-May | Medium | 3/4 | Large deep pink to light rose flowers in large upright trusses. Vigorous, easy-to-grow plant. |
| Anna Rose Whitney | +5 | Late May | Tall | 4/3 | Rose pink flowers to 4" wide in trusses of 12. Dull olive leaves. Needs room. |
| Betty Wormald | −5 | Mid-May | Medium | 4/3 | Pink, pale-centered flowers heavily spotted on upper petals, very large and flat. Huge dome-shaped truss. |
| Bow Bells g. | 0 | Early May | Low | 3/4 | Pink, cup-shaped flowers appear in loose trusses of up to 7. Rounded, spreading plant is well-clothed in medium green, rounded leaves. New foliage is bronze. |
| Cadis | −15 | Late May | Medium | 4/4 | Fragrant, large, light pink flowers are produced in large flat trusses. Dense foliage. Needs some sun for best bloom production. |
| Conewago g. | −25 | Early April | Low | 3/2 | Small lavender-tinged pink flowers and small foliage on a vigorous, rather open plant. |
| Countess of Derby | −5 | Late May | Medium | 4/3 | Deep pink flowers with reddish spotting on upper petals fade to pale pink. Large rounded truss. Open, spreading plant. Also sold as 'Eureka Maid'. |
| Cynthia | −10 | Early May | Tall | 3/3 | Dark rose fading to lighter pink; 3-inch flowers in conical trusses. Medium to dark green foliage. Plant is compact in sun, more open in shade. |
| Everestianum | −15 | Late May | Tall | 2/3 | Slightly bluish-pink with yellow spots in the throat, the frilled 2-inch flowers come in rounded trusses of 15. Dark green 5-inch leaves cover the vigorous, rounded plant. Rugged and adaptable. |
| Faggetter's Favourite | 0 | Late April | Tall | 5/4 | Fragrant pink-flushed flowers with throat speckled bronze. Dark green 7-inch leaves are carried on a vigorous, upright and spreading plant. Sensitive to hot sun. |
| Jock g. | −5 | Late April | Low | 2/4 | Bell-shaped dark pink flowers are 3" across in trusses of 6-8. Dark green leaves cover the dense, spreading plant. Best growth in sun. |
| Kate Waterer | −10 | Late May | Medium | 2/3 | Dark pink flowers with yellow centers are held in tight trusses. Fairly compact plant with good foliage. |
| Loderi g. | 0 | Early May | Tall | 5/4 | Outstanding group of hybrids in white, blush, or pink; 32 are registered, with 'Loderi King George' the best known. Very large trusses of large, fragrant flowers; leaves up to 8" long. Open plant habit. Need protection from wind and sun. |

Rhododendrons, pink...

| NAME | HARDY TO: | SEASON OF BLOOM | HEIGHT | ARS RATING | CHARACTERISTICS |
|---|---|---|---|---|---|
| Marinus Koster | −10 | Mid-May | Tall | 4/3 | Flowers are 5″ across, pink with brown spotting; dome-shaped truss of 10-12. Shiny dark green 7-inch leaves. |
| Mrs. C. B. van Nes | +5 | Late April | Medium | 2/2 | Almost red buds open to dark pink flowers which fade rapidly to light pink; tall trusses. Fairly open plant with light green leaves. |
| Mrs. Charles E. Pearson | −5 | Mid-May | Tall | 4/4 | Large blush pink and orchid flowers have brown spots on upper petals; large dome-shaped trusses. Vigorous plant, with dark green foliage. |
| Mrs. E. C. Stirling | −5 | Early May | Tall | 4/4 | Frilled blush pink flowers with long, decorative stamens; tall conical truss. Leaves are medium to light green on an upright-spreading plant. |
| Mrs. Furnival | −10 | Late May | Medium | 5/5 | Clear pink flowers with light brown blotch in upper petals; tight dome-shaped trusses. Compact plant. |
| Mrs. G. W. Leak | +5 | Late April | Tall | 4/4 | Deep pink with brown flare on upper petals; large conical trusses. Dull grayish-olive leaves. Sometimes sold as 'Cottage Gardens Pride'. |
| Naomi g. | −10 | Early May | Tall | 4/4 | Outstanding group of hybrids, ten of which have been named. Most are rather irridescent pink with shadings of yellow, lilac, or red. |
| Pink Pearl | −5 | Mid-May | Tall | 3/3 | Rose pink fading to blush in large, tall trusses. Open, rangy growth without some shaping. A very dependable grower and bloomer. |
| Pioneer | −20 | March | Medium | 2/3 | Light pink flowers 1 inch across, freely produced. Small leaves are replaced by new each spring. Upright. |
| Praecox g. | −5 | March | Medium | 3/3 | Small rosy-lilac flowers in trusses of 3-4. Compact and upright, with glossy leaves. Can be sheared as a hedge. Very free flowering. |
| Racil | −5 | Early April | Semi-dwarf | 3/2 | Small appleblossom-pink funnel-shaped flowers come in clusters of 3 or 4. A low, mounded plant that is very versatile. |
| Roseum Elegans | −25 | Late May | Tall | 2/4 | Fairly small rosy-lavender flowers are held in domed trusses. Popular as a landscape shrub in cold climates, but is also a good performer in southeast and southwest gardens. Vigorous. |
| Scintillation | −10 | Mid-May | Medium | 4/4 | Large pink flowers with bronze and yellow in the throat are held in a large, domed truss. Large, glossy, dark leaves. Plant needs some shade. |

## RHODODENDRONS (Red)

| NAME | HARDY TO: | SEASON OF BLOOM | HEIGHT | ARS RATING | CHARACTERISTICS |
|---|---|---|---|---|---|
| America | −25 | Late May | Medium | 2/2 | Small dark red flowers in ball-shaped truss. Plant is spreading, better shape in full sun. Dull green foliage. |
| Britannia | −5 | Late May | Medium | 4/4 | Crimson to scarlet flowers in rounded truss. Light dull green leaves; spreading, compact plant. |
| Caractacus | −25 | June | Medium | 1/3 | Purplish-red flowers, excellent compact plant. Foliage may yellow in the sun. |
| Cornubia g. | +15 | Late Winter | Tall | 4/3 | Large blood-red flowers in conical trusses. Medium green leaves on a rapid-growing, upright plant. |

Rhododendrons, red . . .

| NAME | HARDY TO: | SEASON OF BLOOM | HEIGHT | ARS RATING | CHARACTERISTICS |
|------|-----------|-----------------|--------|------------|-----------------|
| David | +5 | Early May | Tall | 4/3 | Dark blood red flowers with contrasting white anthers; upright, loose truss. Dark green leaves on an upright plant. |
| Doncaster | −5 | Late May | Semi-dwarf | 2/3 | Bright crimson-scarlet flowers, 2½ inches across, appear in rounded trusses. Dark green 6-inch leaves on a spreading plant. Tolerates some heat. |
| Dr. V. H. Rutgers | −15 | Late May | Medium | 2/3 | Fringed aniline red flowers. Dark green leaves clothe the broad, dense plant. |
| Earl of Athlone | 0 | Late April | Medium | 5/2 | Striking bell-shaped blood red flowers come in compact, domed trusses. Open, spreading plant with dark green leaves. |
| Elizabeth g. | 0 | Mid-April | Low | 4/4 | Trumpet-shaped red flowers 3½" wide in clusters of 6-8. Dark green leaves on compact, mounded plant. Very free bloomer. |
| Grierosplendour g. | 0 | Late May | Low | 3/3 | Plum colored flowers in a medium sized, rounded truss. Plant is upright when young but becomes rounded and spreading when mature. Young plants bloom profusely. |
| Grosclaude g. | +5 | Late May | Low | 4/4 | Tubular or bell-shaped waxy red flowers in trusses of 9-12. Leaves are dark green with brown indumentum. Slow growth. |
| Holden | −15 | Mid-May | Medium | 3/4 | Rose red flowers with darker red eye come in rounded trusses. Large dark green leaves, compact plant. |
| Ignatius Sargent | −25 | Late May | Medium | 2/2 | Slightly fragrant, large rose-red flowers. Large leaves, open plant. |
| Jean Marie de Montagu | 0 | Mid-May | Medium | 3/4 | Brilliant red flowers in rounded trusses. Attractive dark green foliage. Compact. |
| Kluis Sensation | 0 | Late May | Medium | 3/2 | Dark red flowers produced in small, tight trusses. Leaves are dark green and crinkled. Compact plant. |
| Lady Bligh | 0 | Mid-May | Medium | 4/3 | Strawberry red 3-inch flowers fade to pink with white centers; 10-12 in a rounded truss. Leaves are medium green on a spreading plant. |
| Leo g. | −5 | Mid-May | Medium | 5/3 | Waxy cranberry red flowers in full dome-shaped trusses of 20-24. Dark green leaves to 7" cover the dome-shaped plant. |
| Mars | −10 | Late May | Low to Medium | 4/3 | Deep red with contrasting light stamens; compact, high truss. Plant is slow growing and compact with dark green leaves. |
| May Day g. | +5 | Late April | Low | 4/3 | Bright scarlet trumpets are held in lax trusses on a plant which eventually becomes broader than high. Leaves are 3-4 inches long with tan indumentum. |
| Nova Zembla | −20 | Early May | Medium | 3/3 | Dark red with deeper spots on upper petals. Polished dark leaves, round flower trusses. Good plant habit, adaptable over much of United States. |
| Ruby Bowman | 0 | Early May | Medium | 5/4 | Rose red with red throat, the wavy 4½-inch flowers come in domed trusses of 13-15. Light green leaves are up to 8", clothe the rounded plant to the ground. |
| Trilby | −5 | Late May | Medium | 3/3 | Dark red with blackish center in ball-shaped truss. Leaves are gray to olive green, large, on compact plant. |
| Unknown Warrior | +5 | Mid-April | Medium | 3/2 | Light red 3-inch flowers in domed trusses. Flowers need sun protection but plant is leggy in shade. Upright, open plant; early training pays off. Dark green 6-inch leaves. Good in warm climate. |

## RHODODENDRONS (Blue and Purple)

| NAME | HARDY TO: | SEASON OF BLOOM | HEIGHT | ARS RATING | CHARACTERISTICS |
|------|-----------|-----------------|--------|------------|-----------------|
| A. Bedford | −5 | Late May | Tall | 4/3 | Warm blue with dark blotch on upper petal. Flowers 3¼" across in dome-shaped truss. Tall, vigorous plant. |
| Anah Kruschke | −10 | June | Medium | 2/3 | Lavender-blue flowers in large, tight conical trusses. Compact plant with dark green foliage. Does well in sun. |
| Barto Blue | +5 | April | Tall | 4/3 | Fine quality blue color; trusses of 3 flowers face outward. Tall, upright plant. Leaves to 3". |
| Bluebird g. | 0 | Mid-April | Semi-dwarf | 5/3 | Many small blue flowers on compact, spreading plant. Leaves less than 2" long. Best in sunny location. |
| Blue Diamond g. | 0 | Mid-April | Low | 5/4 | Profuse intense blue flowers on upright, compact plant. Leaves about 1" long. Best in sunny spot. |
| Blue Ensign | −10 | Late May | Medium | 4/4 | Lavender-blue with black spot, 6-9 flowers in a rounded truss. Glossy dark green leaves; upright, spreading plant which tolerates sun. |
| Blue Jay | −5 | Early June | Medium | 4/3 | Lavender-blue flowers with brown blotch; compact, conical truss. Compact plant with large, bright green leaves. |
| Blue Peter | −10 | Early May | Medium | 4/3 | Frilled lavender-blue flowers with purple blotch; conical truss. Spreads wider than high, takes sun. |
| Blue Tit g. | 0 | Mid-April | Semi-dwarf | 4/4 | Small light blue to grayish-blue flowers cover the compact, low plant. Dense green, 1-inch leaves. |
| Caroline | −15 | Mid-May | Tall | 3/3 | Fragrant orchid-lavender flowers are especially long-lasting. Large, long, waxy leaves have wavy margins. |
| Fastuosum Plenum | −10 | Late May | Tall | 3/3 | Semi-double 2-inch flowers are lavender-blue in full trusses. Leaves are dull dark green above, light green below. Plant takes full sun but flowers need part shade. Vigorous. |
| Lee's Dark Purple | −5 | Late May | Medium | | Large trusses of dark purple flowers are held against dark wavy foliage. Good in Southwest. |
| Marchioness of Lansdowne | −15 | June | Medium | 3/3 | Light rose-violet flowers with blackish blotches come in tight dome-shaped trusses. Somewhat open, spreading plant. |
| Parsons Gloriosum | −25 | Late May | Medium | 2/2 | Lavender flowers with pink shadings; truss is compact and conical. Dark leaves, compact plant. |
| Purple Splendour | −10 | Late May | Medium | 4/3 | Considered the finest dark purple, ruffled with a black blotch on upper petals. Compact. |
| Ramapo | −25 | Mid-April | Dwarf | 3/4 | Bright, light violet small flowers are in pleasing contrast to the small grayish-green foliage. Plant is neat, spreading but compact. |
| Russautinii g. | −5 | Mid-April | Medium | 4/3 | Blue to purplish 1-inch flowers are freely produced on an upright shrub. Leaves are medium green, 1 inch long. |
| Sapphire | 0 | Mid-April | Dwarf | 4/4 | Small azalea-like flowers of a bright, light blue. Small aromatic leaves have slight bluish cast. Spreading and dense in sun, taller and more open in shade. |
| Van Nes Sensation | 0 | Early May | Medium | 3/4 | Fragrant pale lilac shading to a white center, 4" across; very large, domed truss. Spreading plant of medium compactness. |

# RHODODENDRONS (Yellow Shades)

| NAME | HARDY TO: | SEASON OF BLOOM | HEIGHT | ARS RATING | CHARACTERISTICS |
|------|-----------|-----------------|--------|------------|-----------------|
| Broughtonii Aureum | 0 | Late May | Low | 3/2 | A rhododendron-azalea hybrid. Soft yellow flowers with orange spots appear in small, rounded trusses. Leaves are thin, 4" long, and semi-deciduous. Plant is sprawling, better where summers are warm. A good southern California plant. |
| Butterfly | 0 | Mid-May | Medium | 3/3 | Large light yellow flowers spotted red in throat; compact, rounded truss. Grows well in sun or shade. |
| Carita g. | +5 | Late April | Medium | 4/4 | Light yellow in trusses of 12-13, domed to flat-topped. Needs sun protection; shy bloomer when young. Several named clones are sold. |
| C.I.S. | +10 | Mid-May | Medium | 4/2 | Funnel-shaped 4-inch flowers are orange-yellow with brilliant red throat; loose, medium-sized trusses. Undulating, 6-inch leaves. Must have light shade. |
| Cowslip g. | 0 | Early April | Low | 3/2 | Bell-shaped flowers of primrose to cream, flushed pink. Plant is low and mounded with oval leaves less than 3" long. |
| Crest | −5 | Early May | Tall | 5/3 | Large trusses of 12 yellow flowers, each 4" wide. Glossy, oval leaves which are held for one year only. |
| Devonshire Cream | 0 | Early May | Semi-dwarf | 3/4 | Creamy yellow flowers with a red basal blotch come in ball-shaped, compact trusses. Dark green 2-inch leaves. Plant is very slow growing and compact. |
| Fabia g. | +10 | Mid-May | Low | 3/3 | A number of named clones from this group are sold; most are in shades of orange, but colors range from pink to vermillion. Lax trusses. Plants are compact, leaves have red-brown indumentum. |
| Goldfort | −10 | Mid-May | Tall | 4/3 | Light yellow flowers with pink and green tints; medium-sized, rounded trusses. Upright and open plant. |
| Harvest Moon | 0 | Early May | Medium | 3/3 | Pale lemon 3½-inch flowers are lightly spotted red; trusses are rounded and compact. Shiny yellow-green leaves; upright plant. |
| Idealist g. | +5 | Late April | Medium | 4/3 | Wide bell-shaped pale yellow flowers are tinted green, in trusses of 10-12. Medium to dark green leaves; upright plant. Needs some shade. |
| King of Shrubs | +5 | Late May | Medium | 4/2 | Apricot yellow with rose shadings; lax trusses display these large flowers. The open plant with light green leaves grows wider than tall. Prefers afternoon shade. |
| Moonstone g. | −5 | Mid-April | Semi-dwarf | 4/4 | Bell-shaped creamy yellow flowers open pink, in lax trusses of 3-5. Leaves are oval, flat, and medium green, about 2½" long. Compact mounded plant prefers afternoon shade. |
| Mrs. Betty Robertson | +5 | Early May | Low | 3/3 | Pale yellow spotted red on upper petals; medium-sized flowers are carried in compact, dome-shaped truss. Dark green leaves, compact shrub which prefers some shade. |
| Souvenir of W. C. Slocock | −5 | Early May | Low | 3/3 | Tight conical trusses of apricot flowers which change to light yellow. Medium green, 4-inch leaves; compact, upright but spreading plant. Slow growth. |
| Unique | +5 | Mid-April | Low | 3/5 | Red buds open to pale yellow flowers flushed peach, in dome-shaped trusses. A first-class landscape shrub: neat, symmetrical, compact, with 3-inch oval leaves. |
| Yellow Hammer | +10 | April | Medium | 4/3 | Very small leaves and flowers. Blooms are bright yellow in clusters of three; leaves are light green. Will take full sun in Northwest. |

## EVERGREEN AZALEAS (White)

| NAME | TYPE | SEASON OF BLOOM | EXPOSURE | CHARACTERISTICS |
|---|---|---|---|---|
| Alaska (Snowbank) | R | Fall-April | Half sun | White, semi-double, with chartreuse blotch. Some flowers are single or double. |
| Everest | Gl | May | Half sun | White flowers with chartreuse blotch. |
| Fielder's White | Sl | February-May | Half to full sun | Frilled single white flowers with faint chartreuse blotch. |
| Glacier | Gl | March-April | Half sun | Large shining white, single flowers; glossy leaves. |
| Gumpo | Mac | May-June | Quarter sun | Large single white flowers. Low, dense plant. |
| Helen Close | ·GL | April-May | Half sun | Large white flowers have pale yellow blotch. Small, dark leaves on a compact, twiggy plant. |
| Madonna | Br | February-April | Half sun | Double white flowers. Rapid, bushy growth with lush leaves. |
| Mme. Petrick Alba | Bl | September-April | Half sun | White semi-double flowers; slow, compact plant. |
| Niobe | Bl | February-April | Half sun | Double flowers of white with chartreuse tinge. |
| Perle de Swynaerde | Bl | Fall-April | Quarter sun | Large double white flowers with contrasting deep green foliage. |
| Purity | R | January-March | Quarter sun | White flowers are single to semi-double, hose-in-hose. |
| Rose Greeley | G | February-May | Half sun | Fragrant hose-in-hose flowers are white wth chartreuse blotch. |
| Snow | K | March-April | Half sun | White hose-in-hose flowers; dead blooms hang on. Upright growth. |
| Snowbird | Sl | January-April | Half to full sun | Fragrant single white flowers with cream to green centers. |
| Sun Valley | GC | March-May | Half sun | Large hose-in-hose flowers are shiny white with green throats. |
| White April | Sl | February-March | Half to full sun | Large single white flowers; upright growth. |

## EVERGREEN AZALEAS (Variegated)

| NAME | TYPE | SEASON OF BLOOM | EXPOSURE | CHARACTERISTICS |
|---|---|---|---|---|
| Albert and Elizabeth | Bl | October-May | Half sun | White with pink edge; double. Rangy plant. |
| California Sunset | Bl | Fall-Spring | Half sun | White and deep pink flowers. |
| Charles Encke | Sl | April-May | Half to full sun | Single white flowers with salmon pink stripes. |
| Eric Schame | Bl | February-March | Quarter sun | Double pink flowers with white edges. |
| Geisha | Gl | February-March | Half sun | Flowers are white, striped red. |
| Iveryana | Sl | April-May | Half to full sun | Single flowers are white with orchid streaks. |
| Professor Wolters | Bl | March-April | Half sun | Single flowers are salmon-rose with white edges. |

## EVERGREEN AZALEAS (Pink)

| NAME | TYPE | SEASON OF BLOOM | EXPOSURE | CHARACTERISTICS |
|---|---|---|---|---|
| Aphrodite | Gl | March-April | Full sun | Pale rose pink. Spreading plant with dark leaves. |
| Avenir | Bl | Fall-Spring | Quarter sun | Copper pink double flowers. Large round leaves. |
| Ballerina | M | March-April | Half sun | Baby pink single flowers; compact plant. |
| Caroline Gable | G | March-April | Half sun | Shocking pink hose-in-hose flowers. |
| Coral Bells | K | Spring | Half sun | Small, single shell pink flowers; small leaves. |
| Duc de Rohan | Sl | March-May | Half sun | Salmon pink single flowers. |
| Fred Sanders (Mrs. Frederick Sanders) | Bl | Fall-Spring | Half sun | Double salmon pink flowers. |
| George Lindley Taber | Sl | March-May | Full sun (if kept moist) | Large light pink single flowers with darker blotch. |
| Gumpo Pink | Mac | May-June | Quarter sun | Single rose-pink flowers with deeper flecks. Low, dense plant. |
| Jean Haerens | Bl | February-May | Half sun | Large, double deep rose pink flowers. |
| L. J. Bobbink | R | March-April | Half sun | Single orchid pink frilled flowers. |
| Louise Gable | G | April-May | Half to full sun | Semi-double pink flowers with darker blotch. Low plant. |
| Macrantha Single Salmon | Mac | Summer | Half sun | Deep salmon flowers. |
| Mme. Pericat (Pink Charm) | P | February-April | Quarter sun | Hose-in-hose light pink flowers with some red markings. |
| Paul Schame | Bl | October-April | Half sun | Large, double salmon pink flowers. |
| Pinkie | Br | April | Little sun | Double light pink flowers. Small, compact plant. |
| Pink Pearl | Bl | Fall-April | Half sun | Soft pink, large double flowers. Upright, slightly open plant. |
| Rosaeflora (Balsaminaeflorum) | Mac | April-May | Little sun | Rose pink double flowers have buds that look like small roses. |
| Rosebud | G | March-April | Half sun | Small, double rose pink flowers. Compact plant, poor in climate extremes. |
| Rose Queen | R | February-April | Half sun | Rose pink flowers are semi-double, hose-in-hose. Upright growth. |
| Southern Charm (Judge Solomon) | Sl | February-April | Half sun | Large single watermelon pink flowers. Plant is open, sprawling, with very large leaves. |
| Sweetheart Supreme | P | February-March | Half sun | Blush pink, semi-double hose-in-hose flowers. |
| Sweet Sixteen | Bl | Fall-April | Half sun | Semi-double light orchid pink flowers. |
| Twenty Grand | P | February-April | Half to full sun | Rose pink semi-double hose-in-hose flowers. |

## EVERGREEN AZALEAS (Red)

| NAME | TYPE | SEASON OF BLOOM | EXPOSURE | CHARACTERISTICS |
|------|------|------------------|----------|-----------------|
| Brilliant | SI | March-May | Full sun (if kept moist) | Carmine red single flowers. |
| Buccaneer | GI | April-May | Half to full sun | Bright orange-red flowers; upright plant. |
| Chimes | BI | Fall-Spring | Half sun | Rich red semi-double, bell-shaped flowers. |
| Dorothy Gish | R | February-April | Quarter sun | Brick red hose-in-hose flowers. Compact plant with dark, glossy leaves. |
| Dr. Bergman | BI | February-March | Quarter sun | Semi-double orange-red flowers. Slow growth. |
| Firelight | R | February-April | Half sun | Bright cherry red hose-in-hose flowers. |
| Flame Creeper | Mac | April-May | Half sun | Single orange-red flowers. Low, spreading plant. |
| Glamour | GL | April-May | Half sun | Large, brilliant rose red flowers. Narrow, dark green leaves. |
| Glory of Sunninghill | SI | April-May | Half to full sun | Vivid orange-red single flowers. |
| Hexe | K | March-May | Half sun | Crimson red, single hose-in-hose flowers. |
| Hino-Crimson | K | February-April | Half to full sun | Brilliant red single flowers cover flat, tiered branches. |
| Hinodegiri | K | February-April | Half to full sun | Cerise red single flowers cover flat, tiered branches. Dark glossy leaves are red in winter. |
| L. C. Bobbink | BI | February-April | Half sun | Large, frilled red semi-double flowers. |
| Lentegroute | BI | February-March | Half sun | Large crimson hose-in-hose flowers. |
| Miss Cottage Gardens | BI | Fall-March | Half sun | Semi-double to double red flowers; compact plant. |
| Mme. Alfred Sanders | BI | October-May | Half sun | Large, double red flowers; compact plant. |
| Mme. Memoria Sander | BI | Fall-April | Half sun | Brilliant rose red double flowers; compact plant. |
| Mme. Petrick | BI | February-April | Half sun | Cherry red semi-double flowers. Plant is low, compact. |
| Pride of Dorking | SI | March-April | Full sun (if kept moist) | Brilliant carmine red flowers; upright, compact plant. |
| Prince of Wales | SI | February-April | Full sun | Rose red single or semi-double flowers. Upright plant. |
| Queen Astrid | BI | December-April | Half sun | Deep orange double flowers. |
| Red Poppy | BI | October-May | Half sun | Huge single dark red flowers. |
| Redwing | P | February-April | Half sun | Red semi-double hose-in-hose flowers; loose plant. |
| Sherwood Red | K | February-April | Half sun | Brilliant orange-red single flowers. Plant is deciduous in very cold weather. |
| Ward's Ruby | K | February-April | Half to full sun | Brilliant dark red small single flowers. |

## EVERGREEN AZALEAS (Lavender and Violet)

| NAME | TYPE | SEASON OF BLOOM | EXPOSURE | CHARACTERISTICS |
|------|------|-----------------|----------|-----------------|
| Constance | R | March-April | Half sun | Large, single, frilled lavender-pink flowers. Light green leaves. |
| Formosa (Phoenicia, Coccinea, Vanessa) | Sl | March-April | Half to full sun | Fluorescent, large, single lavender-pink flowers. Vigorous, rangy plant. |
| Purple Splendor | G | March-April | Half sun | Frilled red-violet flowers with darker blotch, single hose-in-hose. Spreading plant. |
| Sherwood Orchid | K | March-April | Half sun | Large single red-violet flowers with darker blotch. |
| Shinnyo-No-Tsuki | Mac | April-May | Half sun | Large single flowers, violet-red with white centers. |
| Violacea | Bl | February-April | Half sun | Large, double rich violet-purple flowers. Loose plant needs pinching for best shape. |

## DECIDUOUS AZALEAS

| NAME | TYPE | SEASON OF BLOOM | CHARACTERISTICS |
|------|------|-----------------|-----------------|
| Adrian Koster | M | Late May | Deep pure yellow; large, 4-inch flowers. |
| Balzac | Ex | Late May | Fragrant star-shaped orange-red blooms; 12-14 to a truss. |
| Beaulieu | Ex | Late May | Deep pink buds open to soft pink flowers with orange on upper petal. |
| Berryrose | Ex | Early June | Fragrant pale pink flowers with orange centers. New leaves are hairy and bronze-tinted. |
| Brazil | Ex | Early June | Flowers of bright tangerine red with frilled edges. Smaller blooms than some, but many of them. |
| Cecile | Ex | May-early June | Deep pink buds opening salmon pink with a yellow flare. Up to 12 flowers in a truss. Good fall foliage. |
| Christopher Wren | M | Late May | Large chrome yellow flowers with tangerine blotch. |
| Coccinea Speciosa | Gh | Early June | Flowers are orange with a yellowish-orange blotch. |
| Delicatissima | Oc | Late May | Flowers are creamy white flushed rose, with yellow blotch on upper petal. |
| Exquisita | Oc | Late May | Fragrant, white flushed pink flowers have orange throats. |
| Dr. Jacobi | M | Early June | Deep red, $4\frac{1}{2}$-inch flowers. |
| Fireball | Kn | May-early June | Unusually deep red, small flowers and bronze-green foliage. |
| Flamingo | Kn | Late April-May | Frilled flamingo pink flowers on a strong plant. |
| George Reynolds | Ex | Late May | Large flowers of butter yellow with deep gold blotches, green throat. |
| Gibraltar | Ex | Late May | Big flowers with ruffled edges; deep orange flushed with red. Compact shrub. |

**Deciduous azaleas...**

| NAME | TYPE | SEASON OF BLOOM | CHARACTERISTICS |
|------|------|-----------------|-----------------|
| Ginger | Ex | Early June | Round tight trusses of bright tangerine flowers. |
| Golden Dream | Ex | Early June | Golden yellow flowers with orange blotches. Rounded compact clusters of 9-11 flowers. |
| Golden Sunset | Ex | Late May | Unusually large flowers of buff-yellow with orange flare. |
| Goldfinch | Kn | Late May | Apricot yellow flowers shading to pink. Tall grower. |
| Graciosa | Oc | Late May | Orange-yellow flowers have a red suffusion and a tangerine orange blotch. |
| Hotspur Red | Ex | Late May | Very large trusses of orange-red flowers touched yellow on upper petals. |
| Irene Koster | Oc | Late May | Fragrant white flowers flushed deep pink. |
| Knap Hill Red | Kn | Early June | Small flowers of a brilliant deep red. Bronze leaves on a vigorous plant. |
| Koster's Brilliant Red | M | Early June | Blazing orange-red 2½-inch flowers. |
| Lemonora | M | Late May | Flowers are apricot yellow, shaded pink. |
| Magnifica | Oc | Late May | Rose red with orange-yellow blotch. |
| Marina | Ex | Late May | Very large pale yellow flowers with pink shadings. |
| Marion Merriman | Kn | Late May | Rich yellow flowers with deeper yellow flare. |
| Nancy Waterer | Gh | Late May | Large golden yellow flowers. |
| Nicolaas Beets | M | Late May | Apricot to orange-yellow, shaded buff yellow. |
| Oxydol | Ex | Late May | Very large white flowers with yellow blotch in throat. Free flowering plant with bronzy leaves. |
| Princess Royal | Ex | May | Huge, fragrant ivory blooms faintly flushed pink open from pink buds. |
| Renne | Ex | Late May | Rich red flowers suffused with yellow. One of the earliest reds to bloom. |
| Rosella | Kn | Early June | Well-formed large pale pink flowers; fragrant. Strong grower. |
| Royal Lodge | Ex | June | Very deep red flowers with long, decorative stamens. Very late. |
| Spek's Orange | M | June | Fragrant poppy red flowers have a greenish blotch. |
| Strawberry Ice | Ex | May | Frilled trusses of coral pink flowers with yellow flare on upper petals; 11-13 blooms to a truss. |
| Sun Chariot | Ex | Early June | Soft apricot yellow flowers on a compact, spreading plant. |
| Sylphides | Kn | Late May | Very light pink flowers with yellow shadings in the center. |
| Toucan | Kn | May-early June | Large, fragrant creamy-white flowers with big yellow flare. |
| Whitethroat | Kn | Late May | Fragrant pure white double flowers. Compact plant has light green foliage. Flowers are smaller than most, but there are many of them. |

# Index

# PHOTOGRAPHERS

P. J. BRYDON: 10 (left); TOM BURNS, JR.: 14, 41 (bottom); GLENN CHRISTIANSEN: front cover, 42, 46, 47 (left); NANCY DAVIDSON: 4; DONALD C. DAVIS: 67 (top); LYN DAVIS: 17, 40; PHILIP EDINGER: 13 (top, bottom right), 27; RICHARD FISH: 41 (top), 49; JEANETTE GROSSMAN: 7, 10 (right), 16, 24, 44 (top left, bottom), 45; ART HUPY: 6, 43 (left), 54; TATSUO ISHIMOTO: 48 (all); ROY KRELL: 34, 43 (right); DON NORMARK: 8, 9, 12 (all), 21, 62 (top, center), 63 (all), 64, 67 (bottom); PETER REDPATH: 32, 35; JOHN ROBINSON: 11, 15; DAVID H. SWANLUND: 50; ERIC WALTHER: 13 (bottom left); DARROW M. WATT: 47 (right), 53 (all), 60 (all), 62 (bottom); S. C. WILSON: 44 (top right).